Moon

Manifesting

The ultimate guide to manifesting your deepest desires by harnessing the energy of the moon.

By Kyra Howearth

First published in 2021 by Kyra Howearth.

© Kyra Howearth, 2021

This book is dedicated to:

My husband, Dustin, for his never-ending encouragement, love & support,

And my cat & familiar, Snowy, for all her wisdom & strength.

Table of Contents

How I Started Loving The Moon

"Think in the morning. Act in the noon. Read in the evening. And sleep at night."
– William Blake

It makes sense to follow the cycles of nature. We follow the cycles of day & night. We follow the seasons as we move through the cycle of the year. Historically, the moon phase was considered important for fishing and growing crops – and this method is still used by some modern farmers to determine the best times for sowing or harvesting. Ancient calendars from China, Rome and Greece were based on the moon cycle.

So, following the moon cycle to manifest our goals can feel like an ancient practice. It's not so different than farmers sowing seeds at the new moon, nurturing the plants through many moon cycles, and harvesting the crops on the full moon (albeit many moon cycles later).

By tracking the moon, we can also plan ahead to know how we're likely to feel. The moon rules our emotions, so the changes in the moon phases can affect our moods & feelings. Wouldn't it be great to know in advance when you'll be feeling introverted, or inspired, or energetic, or tired?

Sure, to some it might not make logical sense. In fact, many years ago, I would have dismissed the idea of "moon manifesting" entirely because I was such a sceptic. But the moon gives us a framework, a guide to follow. The moon cycle reminds you when it's time to set new goals, take action, or when to relax & recharge.

My goal for writing Moon Manifesting is to help you understand how to work with this framework to manifest your goals. When you align your energy with this natural cycle, when you shift into this flow of energy instead of resisting it, your life will change. Things will become easier. You'll feel less stressed and more in control. Clarity, inspiration & CHANGE will come to you.

So, how did I begin manifesting with the moon?

My fascination with the moon started, like some of you, when I was a child. I can remember many nights when I would stare at the moon, curious about her phases, her craters, or where the moon even came from.

I remember many nights staring out my bedroom window, amazed at how orange the moon appeared on particular nights, or how it seemed to disappear on other nights. Some nights it would seem so BIG and so near to us, whereas other nights the moon would seem like a distant ball of glowing chalk.

The moon was a source of comfort. A glimpse of the moon in the night sky helped me feel supported & nurtured, even from a young age. Looking back, I'm sure there were many nights that my mother sent me to bed – and like any other kid, I did NOT want to go to bed – and in my frustration & sadness that I couldn't stay up and play, the moon shone through my window to soothe me.

Back then, I guess I knew on some subconscious level that the moon symbolized the cycles of life. The moon promised a new day would begin tomorrow. The moon moves through many phases, but she is always whole.

As I became a mother, my awareness increased about how the moon cycle influenced my little family. I saw connections between the moon cycle and my pregnancies & my menstrual cycle. I saw how the full moon influenced the emotions of my family. Babies would be a bit more fussy during the full moon, and the older kids would be restless.

I practiced moon gardening, using the moon as a guide for the best times for sowing seeds, harvesting, or weeding. At first, I wasn't really sure that moon gardening was making a huge difference to my garden, but it gave me encouragement & inspiration for working in my garden. Honestly, before I realised that the waning moon was best for weeding, pruning & mulching, I actually spent very little time on these tasks. But through moon gardening, I found more balance. I focused on growth during the waxing moon, then cleared space in the garden during the waning moon, so I would be ready to sow seeds again on the new moon.

I began to see how the moon could influence other factors in my life, which led me to discovering moon manifesting. It made so much sense – the lunar cycle affects everything from water & plants, to human emotions & sensitivity.

I started setting my intentions with each new moon. I would make time during each new moon to acknowledge what I wanted to bring into reality – what I had been daydreaming about lately, what opportunities had presented in my life, and what I consciously wanted to manifest. This was also when I began to read tarot cards – I'd pull 3 cards each new moon to give me a bit of guidance for the moon cycle ahead.

Through moon manifesting practices, I began to have a spiritual awakening and have new interests. I started believing in tarot & astrology, and I felt that there was something more to life – the Universe, God, or some other Higher Being.

You see, I went to church sometimes when I was a kid, and I loved the idea of praying to God, knowing that He loves us. But as I grew older, I lost my faith in Christianity, and was faithless for many years. When I began my moon manifesting practice, it helped me find faith again -- in the Universe. Setting these new moon intentions felt like a prayer to the Universe.

Through consistently following this new moon ritual, I began to establish meaningful, powerful goals. I began to find out who I was. I had more purpose in my life. I began to follow my own interests and take regular time to do something for ME. I began to dream big & realize my greater potential. I had faith!

This new moon ritual literally changed my entire life.

Moon manifesting was the gateway for me to find faith & spirituality. I was no longer a sceptic, and I began to see how maybe – just maybe – everything was connected, maybe the tarot cards I pulled out weren't just a "coincidence", maybe there was some Higher Being that could help me transform my life and became the best version of myself.

So, I don't know if it's because I started to BELIEVE and have faith, or if it was something else that I was doing right, but I began to regularly manifest my goals. I set intentions to start up my business, then I manifested not one, but TWO amazing opportunities to rent office spaces with complementary therapists. I set intentions to buy our first house, and I'm now living in the EXACT house I wrote down into my moon journal.

Looking back on intentions I set years ago, I've manifested a lot of my intentions – some just took a bit of extra time, and some manifested in a different way than I expected. Trying to manifest a new computer meant that unfortunately, my old computer had to inconveniently fail in the process. I needed a replacement, and fast, so I bought a new one with my credit card. Did I really think that I would somehow receive a brand new computer with all my desired specifications, delivered to my doorstep, all for FREE? Lesson learnt: the Universe works in mysterious ways – next time, be more clear!

Here's another quick moon manifesting story for you.

When I was heavily pregnant with my 4th baby, one of my new moon intentions was to find a 7-seater car so the whole family would fit. I just wanted something cheap but spacious enough so we could all fit in when the baby arrived. So, imagine my surprise when I randomly drove past a 7-seater Pajero selling for $3000! This was a pretty low price, especially for a big four-wheel drive. I called my husband to mention where the car was, and if he drove past it, could he have a look? Well, about 30 minutes later, my husband drove down our driveway in this 7-seater Pajero.

I couldn't believe this manifested so quickly!

Moon manifesting works. It has made such a difference to my entire life – not only with manifesting physical desires, such as a car, but also to create a sense of emotional, mental & spiritual wellbeing. Aligning your energy to the moon cycle can really transform your life. By following the moon, so many doors have opened up for me – doors that I never even realized existed.

Moon manifesting works when you follow the process. Having faith that your intentions will manifest is essential, and almost as important as the goal itself – if you don't BELIEVE your desired outcome will manifest, then it's unlikely that it will. Believe that the process will work – and it will.

Over the years, I've taught moon manifesting through numerous full moon + new moon circles in my local area, as well as a range of online and in-person spiritual workshops, courses & an amazing retreat in Bali. I publish an annual moon planner, making it super easy to align your daily life with the moon.

Just like all my goals, this book started as a new moon intention. I wanted to create an easy-to-understand and actionable guide so you can harness the energy of the moon in each of her phases in a practical way. My mission is to help you find more purpose & transform your life with the moon.

Over many moon cycles, this book slowly came to life. I nurtured that seed of intention and manifested this book by working tightly with the moon cycle. This book is proof that working with the moon cycle can help you manifest your biggest goals!

So, welcome to Moon Manifesting! It is my deepest desire that this book inspires you to dream big & to manifest your goals with the power of the moon. I'm so excited for you!

Kyra x

How To Use This Book

"Aim for the moon.
If you miss, you may hit a star."
– W. Clement Stone

Welcome to your journey of manifesting with the moon! I've created this book to be used as a practical guidebook to working with the moon cycle. Ideally, you can pick this book up at any point in the moon cycle, find the relevant sections, and quickly understand how to work with the current energy of the moon cycle.

Working with the moon can be a daily practice. I always incorporate the moon into my daily activities and use the moon as my constant guide for how to spend my energy. At the minimum, if you check in with the moon once a week that will help you align your energy with the moon phase.

If you're feeling stuck at any point and don't know what you should be doing to manifest with the moon, it can be useful to ask tarot or oracle cards for guidance. You might like to ask your cards about what action you need to take or what's stopping you from manifesting your goals. I've included questions to ask the cards for each moon phase. The cards can bring clarity & guidance, but always trust your intuition when making decisions & taking action. The cards are just a prompt for your own intuitive knowing.

For each moon phase, you'll also find journal prompts & practical action steps. I highly recommend starting a journal to record the moon phase & sign each day, how you're feeling, what you're working on, and anything else you want to include about your moon manifesting journey. It's so handy to have all your new moon intentions in one place so you can easily flip back and check in on your intentions!

So let this book guide you through creating your own moon practice. No matter the day, you can open this book to the current moon phase (and also the current zodiac sign the moon is in) and find your guidance for the day ahead.

When you're ready to go deeper, you can learn about your own moon sign, eclipses, and void-of-course moons. There is lots of information in this book to guide you through ANY moon phase and tips on using the moon as your personal guide. If it's too overwhelming, just go back to the basics – what's the moon phase & zodiac sign today? This simple daily practice will become a valued source of guidance.

INTRODUCTION

All About The Moon & Manifesting

"It was lunar symbolism that enabled man to relate and connect such heterogeneous things as: birth, becoming, death, and resurrection; the waters, plants, woman, fecundity, and immortality; the cosmic darkness, prenatal existence, and life after death, followed by the rebirth of the lunar type..."
— Mircea Eliade

Understanding the symbolism of the moon is the first thing to learn so you can begin to harness this energy. I've chosen to begin this book with a list of correspondences & associations with the moon, to enable you to see the connections between the lunar energy and life on Earth.

.

MOON CORRESPONDENCES AND ASSOCIATIONS

Day of the week: Monday

Element: water

Gender: feminine

Zodiac: Cancer

Herbs: lemon balm, mugwort, willow, purslane, aloe vera, bladderwrack, chickweed, calamus, marshmallow, Irish moss

Flowers: moonflower, lily, lotus, waterlily, gardenia, camellia, passionflower, poppy

Essential oils: lemon balm, eucalyptus, wintergreen, jasmine, lemon, sandalwood, myrrh

Food: sprouts, lettuce, cucumber, melons, coconut, turnip, potato, papaya

Crystals: moonstone, selenite, opal

Tarot card: XVIII The Moon

Colours: white, silver, shades of grey, cream

Associations: cycles, birth, motherhood, emotions, water

"The moon is a loyal companion. It never leaves. It's always there, watching, steadfast, knowing us in our light and dark moments, changing forever just as we do. Every day it's a different version of itself. Sometimes weak and wan, sometimes strong and full of light. The moon understands what it means to be human. Uncertain. Alone. Cratered by imperfections."
— *Tahereh Mafi*

The moon is our (almost) constant companion in the sky. We often search for her in the night or get a pleasant surprise when we spy her during the day. The moon is easy to track, even for the most novice astronomer or astrologer.

Throughout childhood, we usually observe that the moon has different phases. Some nights the moon is big & bright, impossible to miss. But other nights we need to search the sky for a glimmer of a crescent moon. On other nights, the moon simply isn't there. Then we begin to see the moon during the day, and we question why the moon is out during the daytime.

True story: I didn't actually know how the moon phases were formed until I looked it up so I could teach the moon phases to my 8-year-old son.

So, the moon reflects the light from the sun. The moon is orbiting around the Earth, taking 29.5 days to complete an orbit – this is the moon cycle. The moon phases are created by the angle that the moon is making with the sun as it orbits through the cycle. The moon always has half of its surface illuminated by the sun. It's just our PERSPECTIVE from here on Earth that makes the moon look partially or completely illuminated.

So, when it's the first quarter or last quarter moon, we are looking at the moon "sideways" – seeing an equal amount of the moon illuminated & dark. During the full moon, we are looking at the moon as it makes a 180-degree angle with the sun, fully illuminated. During the new moon, as the moon crosses close to the path of the sun, we can't see the moon as the illuminated side is facing away from the Earth towards the sun.

The following is an activity that I did with my son when he was excited about learning about the moon. Together we tracked the moon on a daily basis, observing the evolution of the moon phase throughout the cycle. I personally learnt a lot about the moon, even though the activity was aimed at kids! It's the perfect place to start when discovering the moon cycle.

ACTIVITY

Track the moon for the month. Each day, observe the moon in the sky. What phase is the moon? Is it waxing (getting fuller) or waning (getting darker)? What time is the moon rising and setting each day? See what else you can observe about the moon as she moves through an entire cycle.

Astrologically, the moon symbolizes our inner emotions, feelings & our intuition. This is why during full moons, we may often feel more emotional or intuitive than usual (although there are lots of other factors regarding how the moon influences us, and you'll discover this as you continue to read).

Have you noticed that you eat more around the full moon? Perhaps you're prone to having a few-too-many drinks when the moon is full? Or maybe you notice other cravings or addictions that come to the surface at this time of the moon cycle. The moon also influences our emotional security – what we need, on an emotional level, to feel safe & secure within ourselves. So, if we are feeling emotionally insecure – for whatever reasons, and in whichever way it shows up in your life – we may see these effects show up more intensely during a full moon.

One of my first explorations of the spiritual meaning of the moon was through exploring the tarot card XVIII The Moon. As I began to learn tarot as part of my new moon rituals, I was really drawn to The Moon card. I'd get excited when I saw The Moon show up in my readings - at the time, I was feeling like it symbolized that I was on the right path by following the moon cycle & honouring the different phases.

In tarot, XVIII The Moon can symbolize aspects of the moon that I've already explained in this book, such as emotions, creativity & intuition. It can also symbolize illusions & deception, and that all is not as it seems. Transformation & evolution through phases is another key interpretation.

One of my favourite quotes about this card comes from The Book of Tarot by Danielle Noel. Danielle says, "It represents an ancient, arcane magic that resides within us all." This quote helps to explain how we can use the moon to manifest magic into our lives. The moon is symbolic of that magic we already have - we just have to learn HOW to use that magic.

So how does the moon have anything to do with manifesting your goals & dreams?

On a spiritual or energetic level, the moon helps us tune into the energies of the Universe as we connect to this natural cycle. This spiritual connection,

5

this faith in some Higher Being, heightens our manifesting abilities because we believe we have a loving & powerful co-creator working with us.

On an emotional level, as the moon influences our moods & emotions, we can learn how to work with this natural cycle so we know when we might be feeling energetic & confident, or when we're more likely to be feeling exhausted. The moon also guides us towards creating more emotional security.

Mentally, working with the moon cycle helps you set realistic goals and use the timeline of the moon to plan for. I personally love setting goals for the 4 weeks ahead at each new moon, and checking in on those goals at the next new moon.

Physically, you're probably already aware of how the moon physically affects life on Earth. You can see the changes in the tides in direct correlation to the moon. So, for manifesting purposes, we can use the moon as a guide for manifesting your physical desires towards you. Isn't life easy when you can naturally attract or magnetize your desired outcome TO you, instead of working really hard?

"Don't worry if you're making waves just by being yourself. The moon does it all the time."
- Scott Stabile

There are so many ways to use the moon as a guide for manifesting. You can use the phases as a guide to determine how to direct your energy. You can follow the moon through the zodiac. As the moon moves through the zodiac, you can use this to guide which body parts or chakras to focus on, which crystals to carry with you, or which activities to focus on.

The great thing about moon manifesting is that it's not all hard work and no fun. Since beginning my moon manifesting journey, I've brought more balance into my life. I prioritize self-care during the waning moon. I get out paints or colour pencils when the moon moves through a creative fire sign. I take regular long baths when the moon is in a water sign, like Pisces, Cancer or Scorpio. I feel that self-care & moon manifesting go hand-in-hand with each other!

The moon's cycle around Earth takes 29.5 days. During this time, the moon moves through 9 distinct phases and all 12 zodiac signs, spending around 2.5 days in each sign.

The 9 moon phases are:
- **New moon**. A time for setting intentions & new beginnings.
- **Waxing crescent.** Plan ahead & dream big, nurturing your new intentions to grow.
- **First quarter.** Take aligned & inspired action towards your intentions.
- **Waxing gibbous.** Push through obstacles & work hard to achieve your goals.
- **Full moon.** Celebrate & appreciate your achievements.
- **Waning gibbous.** Share your successes with others, show gratitude.
- **Last quarter.** Reflect, review & release.
- **Waning crescent**. Let go and surrender to the Universe's will.

- **Balsamic or dark moon.** Go within, meditate, hibernate. Find stillness & solitude.

You'll discover more deeply the energy of each specific phase throughout this book, but hopefully you can already see the energy of the moon cycle.

The moon cycle gives us a framework to manifest with. Knowing how to work with each phase helps you shift into the energetic flow of the Universe. You begin working WITH the cycles of nature, instead of against.

You can add a deeper layer of energy to each moon phase by knowing which zodiac sign the moon is in. The zodiac signs give the moon phase a particular energy – so we know that a new moon is a good time for setting new intentions, but a new moon in Aries will have a different energy than a new moon in Taurus. You'll discover more about the zodiac signs later in this book.

CHAPTER 1

New Moon

Intention Setting Rituals

+ BEGINNINGS + INTENTIONS + SETTING GOALS +

"Moonlight drowns out all but the brightest stars."
- J. R. R. Tolkien

So, when do you feel is the most POWERFUL time of the moon cycle?

I used to think the full moon was the most magickal time of the cycle. Without a doubt, there's something powerful & intense about seeing the fully illuminated moon, casting soft light over the darkness of the world.

But then I started my journey with moon manifesting, and I discovered the power of the new moon. Never underestimate the power of darkness. Without darkness, there would be no light. The new moon is often ignored, but this is a powerful portal for setting intentions for what you desire to manifest.

The new moon marks the beginning of a new cycle. This is the ideal time for setting fresh intentions, making new plans, and bringing new dreams to life. Without dreaming & setting goals, how can we make any progress towards manifesting anything?

The moon is in the new moon phase when the moon is aligned or conjunct with the sun. You won't see the moon at all when the moon is new, as its path will be closely aligned with the path of the sun, making the moon invisible from our perspective on Earth. You can understand why the new moon is often ignored – we can't see it at all!

Despite not being able to actually see the moon during the new moon phase, many agree that this is the most powerful time of the moon cycle. By the time you've finished this chapter, you'll understand why!

In the absence of the light of the moon, we can see the stars more clearly. The night sky on a new moon is an astrological metaphor for letting the stars guide us. Connect with the Universe to guide you through setting new intentions for the moon cycle ahead. The new moon is a potent time for tuning in to your inner self and finding inspiration from within.

The new moon is the best time for getting clear on what you want to manifest. New/full moon cycles come around every 6 (or so) months, so the intentions you set on a particular new moon generally won't manifest until the full moon in the same zodiac sign (which falls around 6 months later). It's like gardening – you need to sow the seeds first, then tend to them with loving care, and over a few months you watch the plant grow until finally you can harvest. The new moon is the ideal time for sowing the seeds of your intentions – and with loving care, commitment & action, you'll eventually manifest these intentions.

During the new moon, you can choose to focus on setting tangible goals, such as receiving $1,000 by a certain date, however I find it more helpful to focus on how I want to feel. So instead of setting my intention as receiving money, I think about how I would FEEL once I had that money. Would more money bring you a feeling of happiness? Security? Abundance? By focusing on the feeling, you can send out a stronger message to the Universe of what you want to manifest. It's then up to the Universe to send you that feeling – but sometimes it manifests in unexpected ways!

New moon journal prompts:
- What have I been daydreaming, fantasizing about, or wishing for recently?
- What is currently inspiring me?
- How would I like to feel this month?
- How would I like to manifest into my life over the next 6 months?
- What are my intentions for this new moon?

Questions to ask the cards on the new moon:
- What is beginning in my life this new moon?
- What will I manifest over these next 6 months?
- What obstacles do I need to be aware of?

Action steps for the new moon:
- **Meditate.** Quieten the mind, bring the mental chatter to stillness. Inspiration comes from these still moments. Meditate before setting

your intentions & goals to find deeper clarity on what you actually want to manifest into your life. If you don't know how to meditate, try a guided meditation. I've made a guided new moon meditation for you to listen to – you can check it out (plus download other bonuses to complement this book) at *HerbalMoonGoddess.com/MoonManifestingBonus*

- **Set your intentions.** This can be as simple or elaborate as you want to make it. Set your intentions while meditating or journaling, or take it further with a symbolic ritual. There's no right or wrong way to set your intentions. The power from setting your intentions comes from how strongly you feel about it & your faith that it will happen.

- **Daydream & find inspiration.** If you don't know WHAT your intentions should be for the month ahead, just take time out to daydream for a while. You may notice your thoughts hold clues about what you truly desire to manifest. Find inspiration from WITHIN, rather than looking around you and manifesting what others have.

CHAPTER 2

Waxing Moon

+ ACTION + INSPIRATION + ENERGY + CREATIVITY + GROWTH +

"I never really thought about how when I look at the moon, it's the same moon as Shakespeare and Marie Antoinette and George Washington and Cleopatra looked at."
— Susan Beth Pfeffer

The waxing moon is when you take action on those plans you started in the new moon period. Initially, we're still downloading our dreams & what steps we actually need to take. At the moon starts to grow, it becomes time to bring these dreams to life + into your reality! For me, this is when the magic really starts to happen.

When I was working on this book, I recall jotting down my ideas around the new moon. Planning out the chapters, brainstorming what needs to be in here, just getting all my thoughts down into a document. Then I remember distinctly the switch of energy around the first quarter moon. All of a sudden it's like "Sh*t! I've got a book to write! I need to expand this 3-page document of brain-dump into an actual BOOK!". The Universe kicked me into gear and suddenly I was motivated + inspired to work consistently towards creating this book. I dedicated late nights & any spare moments towards working on getting this book written. You know when you just get so wrapped up in projects and you just *know* you've got to get it done? You get on a roll, and you don't really care that it's 2am and you're still working away. You just KNOW you've got to get this baby out there.

That's what the waxing moon energy can be like. It energizes you & fuels your creativity. Harness this energy by pushing yourself to take action towards your new moon intentions + goals!

The waxing moon can be broken down into a few distinct phases:
- Waxing crescent
- First quarter
- Waxing gibbous

The main thing to remember is that the waxing moon is a time of growth. The energy is increasing, so you are generally likely to feel more energized too. This is the time to be getting most of your work done (then, you can review & make changes during the waning moon).

Waxing crescent

+ INSPIRATION + PLAN AHEAD + HOPE +

"When hope is fleeting, stop for a moment and visualize, in a sky of silver, the crescent of a lavender moon. Imagine it -- delicate, slim, precise, like a paper-thin slice from a cabochon jewel. It may not be very useful, but it is beautiful. And sometimes it is enough."
— *Vera Nazarian*

The waxing crescent moon describes the beginning of the moon cycle, as the moon's mystical powers begin to awaken. From the darkness of the new moon, the waxing crescent begins to emerge for a short time after sunset. Initially, you can find the waxing crescent moon in the sky just after sunset by looking towards the western horizon. As the waxing crescent grows fuller, the moon will be visible in the western night sky until late. If your bedroom faces west, you may notice the moon shining into your bedroom as you go to bed.

For me, seeing the waxing crescent moon in the sky is like greeting an old friend. Personally, I don't often see the moon during the waning crescent, so I may miss out on seeing the moon for a week or longer around the new moon period. When I do finally catch a glimpse of the waxing crescent, the moon sends inspiration, hope & serenity. A reminder of the natural cycles of life.

Working with the energy of the waxing crescent gives us space to daydream, meditate & plan ahead. We ease ourselves out of the darkness of the new moon sloooowly – there's no need to rush into taking action if you don't feel ready. The waxing crescent allows us to find clarity in what we truly want to manifest, what we truly want our life to look like. Allow yourself to dream big. Get clear on the details. Create a vision board, journal down what your best life looks like, make a step-by-step plan to bring your biggest dreams into reality.

The waxing crescent helps you refine your new moon intentions. So, let's say that you want to manifest a new car, and you've set that intention during the new moon. During the waxing crescent phase, you get to research different cars, figure out the type of car you want, how many seats or doors, what brand, or whatever else you SPECIFICALLY want for your new car.

If you are already super clear on the specifics of what you want to manifest, but don't know HOW you'll ever manifest it, just ask the Universe. The waxing crescent phase can be a great time to use tarot cards, oracle cards, runes, or other forms of guidance from the Universe. If you feel stuck and don't know what your next step is for manifesting your goals – just ask the Universe. Listen to your intuition. This guidance will ALWAYS lead you in the right direction.

Waxing crescent journal prompts:
- What steps do I need to take to bring my dreams & goals into reality?
- How can I plan ahead to ensure I meet my goals?

- What resources, connections or skills will I
  need? What would help me manifest my goals?

**Questions to ask your cards during the waxing
crescent:**
- What is the next step to help me manifest my
  goals?
- What potential obstacles should I plan for?
- What do I need to consider about my goals?

Action steps for the waxing crescent moon:
- **Make a vision board of the goals & dreams
  you're working towards.** Add inspiring photos,
  images, drawings, or anything else that
  reminds you of your dreams. You could add in
  some affirmations in alignment with your new
  moon intentions. An extra magickal step could
  include adding some small crystal chips or a
  few drops of essential oil so amplify the power
  of your vision board.

- **Take a page in your journal to describe in
  detail what your ideal life looks like**. In your
  ideal life, what would your day look like? What
  would you do? What clothes would you wear?
  What food would you eat? What would you do
  for work? Where would you live? Go deep into
  the details to make it easier to manifest.

- **Turn your intentions into SMART goals.**
  SMART is an acronym for specific, measurable,
  achievable, relevant and time-specific. Get
  specific about WHAT you want to manifest – go

right into the fine details of exactly what you're trying to achieve. How will you measure your progress or success? Make your goal actually achievable – is it possible to achieve this? Do you have the necessary skills or tools to achieve your goal? How relevant is your goal to your overall mission? Ensure your goal is in alignment with your true values. Finally, add a timeframe to achieve your goal by. Giving yourself a deadline is a great motivator!

First quarter

+ TAKE ALIGNED ACTION + MAKE YOUR OWN MAGICK +

"Be the moon and inspire people, even when you're far from full."
— K. Tolnoe

The first quarter moon occurs approximately 7 days after the new moon. By now, the moon is rising around midday and setting around midnight. You may note that your energy levels are picking up and you're naturally making good progress towards your goals.

The first quarter marks the switch of energy from the "dreamy" new moon energy to the "let's do it!" waxing moon energy. After taking time to tune into our true desires & intentions, planning ahead with attention to detail, we now feel ready to take action.

It's the time when you take your plans and roll up your sleeves to do the work in order to make it happen.

The thing about manifesting is that often people will send out their prayers, intentions & wishes to the Universe, but...then nothing happens. Yes, sometimes we can get lucky and randomly manifest amazing things out of nowhere. But a lot of the time (okay, most of the time), we need to give a little to get more in return. Action creates results.

So literally – put your plan into action during the first quarter moon. Check in with your goals & intentions from the new moon and take aligned action. Even if it's something small like reaching out to someone, making a phone call, or booking an appointment.

Taking aligned action is where a lot of the magick of manifesting is. We find that somehow, somewhere, deep inside of us is this immense power. We find our potential to show up, do the work, and make things happen!

Taking aligned action is NOT getting busy with your to-do list, but neglecting to do the work that will directly affect your goals. Trust me – you can often get so busy with all these little tasks, and run out of time or energy to work on the stuff that truly matters to you. We often procrastinate – sometimes it's a subconscious thing and we don't even realise we're procrastinating. Identify when you're resisting & procrastinating, and consider what needs to change so you can just get on with taking action.

You might be genuinely busy with lots of responsibilities, maybe juggling kids while working from home and still trying to find time to achieve your goals. Know when to re-prioritize your to-do list – it's okay to let some of the housework come to a standstill so you can dedicate time to the stuff that actually matters to you.

I'll give you an example of what aligned action looks life. If you're attempting to write a book, make dedicated time every day to sit down and actually write it out. Even if it's just 5 or 10 minutes a day – you'll be taking aligned action, and you'll be making tangible progress towards your goals. Soon you'll be in the habit of writing daily, and you'll soon have your book completed. Aligned action isn't just thinking about what you'll write, or procrastinating by cleaning your desk.

When you just don't know WHAT to do to bring your goals to life, ask the Universe or find inspiration elsewhere so you can take INSPIRED action. Sometimes we find inspiration from within – perhaps during meditation, yoga or in the shower. At other times, we find inspiration from the external world. An inspiring post on social media, an interesting article, a conversation with a friend. If you feel stuck, look for inspiration to take you to the next aligned action towards your goals.

First quarter moon journal prompts:
- What action can I take TODAY to bring me closer to my goals?
- What actions do I need to complete over the next week to manifest my goals?
- How can I stay committed towards achieving my goals?

Questions to ask your cards during the first quarter moon:

- What is the Universe currently supporting me with?
- What action do I need to take this week to manifest my goals?
- What's currently stopping me from manifesting my goals?

Action steps for the first quarter moon:

- **Write out a to-do list.** Include all the big & little tasks you need to take action on to reach your goals for this moon cycle. Then do it! Keep taking aligned action towards your goals.

- **Stay focused & productive.** What blocks are coming up that are stopping you from achieving your goals? How do you keep procrastinating? Identify what's holding you back and make the appropriate changes so you can just get on with taking aligned action.

- **Make it easier.** If your to-do list suddenly feels huge & unachievable, considering delegating tasks to others or even taking things OFF your to-do list. I learnt the "automate, delegate or eliminate" rule from one of my mentors, Tammy Guest. If it's not something that you personally need to do, consider how you could automate it – is there technology or systems that could do it for you? Could you outsource the task and delegate it to someone else to do?

Or is it something that NO-ONE actually needs to do – could it be deleted from your to-do list altogether?

Waxing gibbous

+ PUSH THROUGH + CHALLENGE YOURSELF + PHYSICAL ENERGY +

"Life is either a daring adventure
or nothing at all."
- Helen Keller

Roll up your sleeves – there's still work to do! The waxing gibbous moon inspires & energizes us to work hard towards our goals.

The waxing gibbous moon describes the week before the full moon, as the moon grows nearer to 100% illumination. This is a period of high energy – you may need less sleep, and naturally stay up later at night.

The moon rises later throughout the afternoon, setting in the early hours of the morning. You'll often see the moon shining through your windows during the night hours.

With these high energy levels, you'll naturally push yourself. You'll have the energy and strength to overcome any obstacles, resistance or procrastination that stands between you & your goals. You can make a lot of progress towards your goals during the waxing gibbous phase if you stay focused on what you're manifesting.

This is when we do the work. Think of it as meeting the Universe halfway – we send out our intentions & wishes, then we take aligned action. We need to do our share of the work, right? Don't worry, after the full moon we'll get a chance to rest & receive. But right now, during the waxing gibbous moon, is when we need to be really pushing ourselves, working hard towards our goals.

Remember that aligned action I was talking about in the First Quarter Moon section? Take committed & aligned action towards your goals every day. When things feel difficult, know that you're pushing in the right direction so you can advance to the next level. Growth requires us to do difficult things. Don't give up if things feel too hard! Let the moon guide & comfort you as you take each scary (but aligned) step.

The waxing gibbous phase can be a time of adjustment. Our goals haven't manifested yet – but we are making progress! As we work hard, challenging ourselves to keep moving forward towards our dreams, we may need to refine our plans or actions. If things do feel difficult, consider if there's an alternative way. Maybe someone else could help – you could hire a virtual assistant, a book coach, a social media manager, a mentor, or someone else that will help your goals manifest a bit easier. There's no shame in asking for help when we need it – we're not here to do everything on our own.

Reaching out for help or adding someone to your team is such a rewarding challenge. Every time I've done this, I felt sooo nervous about reaching out. *What will they think of me? Will they think I'm weak? Maybe this is a stupid idea!* But most of the time, I get amazing responses that make me feel so supported. And then I wonder to myself, why didn't I do this earlier? Of course, sometimes you get rejected. Don't worry about those rejections – trust that it doesn't work out for a reason. The perfectly aligned opportunity WILL come – just keep making offers, keep reaching out, and the Universe will support you. It doesn't hurt to ask!

The point is, just keep taking steps towards your goals. We don't grow if we stay in our comfort zone. When you get those niggling thoughts like "I'm not good enough to do this" or "No one will like this", know that this is a sign that you are on the edge of growth. Growth is required to achieve your dream goals. So just tell that little voice in your head that it's okay! That it's SAFE to do this – and make that leap out of your comfort zone.

Waxing gibbous journal prompts:
- What obstacles are stopping me from manifesting my goals?
- How can I overcome these obstacles?
- What challenging action step am I resisting? Why am I resisting this?
- What is the single most important thing I could do today that will bring me closer to my goal?

Questions to ask your cards during the waxing gibbous moon:
- What obstacle is blocking me from achieving my goals?

- What challenge do I need to rise to?
- What needs to be refined or adjusted so I can manifest my goals?

Action steps during the waxing gibbous moon:
- **Ask for guidance**. Consult the Universe when you come up against obstacles, challenges or resistance. If you feel stuck and you're not sure what your next step is, ask the Universe. Draw some tarot or oracle cards, meditate, ask your pendulum, or just ask the Universe for a sign. Listen to the advice that comes through and take action accordingly.

- **Keep taking committed & aligned action towards your goals.** This is the time of the cycle when you naturally work hard & push ahead towards your goals. Do the hard work. Take the next step (even if it feels super scary & way out of your comfort zone!). Find courage to take action.

- **Overcome obstacles**. Notice where resistance is coming up for you. If you find yourself procrastinating or feeling that the task at hand is too difficult, figure out how you can overcome this challenge. Don't let little things stop you from manifesting your goals!

CHAPTER 3

Full Moon

+ RELEASE + GRATITUDE + CELEBRATE +
+ FORGIVENESS +

"The moon will guide you through the night with her brightness, but she will always dwell in the darkness, in order to be seen."
— Shannon L. Alder

The full moon lighting up the night sky is a source of endless inspiration. The moon has inspired us for thousands of years. There are countless songs, poems, artworks and books dedicated to the moon.

In this chapter, you'll discover how to harness the energy of the full moon for your own inspiration, creation & manifestation.

The full moon will rise in the sky around sunset, as the moon is directly opposite the sun at this time. The moon will then set at around sunrise.

The moon is fully illuminated at this time. Although we can go into the specifics of when the moon is ACTUALLY full, or when it's in the waxing gibbous or waning gibbous phases, generally you can tap into this full moon energy even if it's not 100% illuminated. I used to make a big deal about doing my full moon rituals at the exact time of 100% illumination, but now I'm much more chilled about it. I'll often doing my full moon ritual the night before or after a full moon if the timing works out better with my other commitments.

Full moons mark the peak energy of the moon cycle. As the moon rules our emotions, feelings & intuition, you may find that you (or people around you) are a bit more upset, angry, crazy or psychic than usual. So, working WITH the moon means that this is an important time of the cycle to honour your feelings. If you're feeling overwhelmed – take a break. If you feel the need to binge eat Ben & Jerry's ice cream while watching reruns of *Friends* – do it. If you're feeling inspired – follow your inspirations & get creative. If you're feeling angry or upset – write in your journal or talk to a friend, explore your emotions.

Because the full moon helps us become more aware of our emotions, the full moon is an ideal time for opening our hearts and practicing gratitude & forgiveness. When we drop out of our mind & into our heart, we have the potential to make big energetic shifts. Releasing emotions – especially emotions that we've held onto for sooooo long – can be especially transformative during a full moon. Allow yourself to let go of grudges you've been holding onto. Release anger, sadness, frustration or other emotions – you may like to journal, talk with a friend, or do a ritual. Cord cutting rituals and fire releasing rituals are some of my favourites!

"The moon is the reflection of your heart and moonlight is the twinkle of your love."
— Debasish Mridha

Gratitude is, at least in my opinion, one of the strongest ways to harness the power of the full moon. Showing gratitude is to show thanks for what you have received in your life. Even though we can be caught in a cycle of always wanting more, we always have enough. There is always enough. The Universe ALWAYS provides. Sometimes we just need to slow down and acknowledge the abundance already present in our lives.

On the full moon, appreciate what you have harvested in your life. Sending out gratitude will show the Universe what you want more of. If you want to manifest money, show gratitude for every single coin that shows up in your life. If you want to manifest your book to be written, show gratitude for all the inspiration & motivation you've received towards writing your book. Manifesting a soul mate? Show gratitude for all the loving relationships in your life.

Forgiveness operates on a similar vibration to gratitude. You see, both gratitude and forgiveness help to open the heart chakra. When we open ourselves to unconditional love, we also open ourselves to receiving abundance & prosperity into our lives. So, forgiveness is another powerful manifesting tool, especially under the heightened energy of the full moon.

Forgive anyone who you've been feeling uncomfortable about. Forgive your parents. Forgive your ex-partners. Forgive that person who left you a negative review. Let go of grudges from the past. We can get so STUCK in our energy when we hold onto emotions from the past. If you want to move forward and manifest something new, you need to let go of the stuff that's holding you back. Forgiveness during the full moon is the perfect way to release & let go.

As the energy of the lunar cycle reaches its peak during the full moon, we can expect the energy of our goals & intentions to do the same. The full moon is typically when our goals come to fruition! We can harvest the fruit of our labours & celebrate our successes. Remember that your new moon intentions may not manifest for about 6 months – so whatever you're harvesting on this full moon is likely to have grown from seeds you planted (literally or figuratively!) 6 months ago.

Be sure to celebrate your wins during the full moon! Show gratitude for all that's manifested into your life. Relax and appreciate all the hard work you've put towards your goals over the past few weeks. You've worked really hard & challenged yourself during the waxing gibbous phase, so now it's time to sit back & celebrate how far you've come!

One of my favourite ways to celebrate during the full moon is by getting together with some like-minded people. When I first started my business, Herbal Moon Goddess, I started out by holding full moon circles in my town. I'd been to a few full moon circles before, but there wasn't anything I could attend locally, so I thought I'd just start hosting my own full moon events. I live in a small country city, and at first I thought there would be hardly anyone interested in attending full moon circles. My first circle was booked out, with over 25 attendees jammed into a small conference room!

Getting together for a full moon circle can be a powerful experience. It's like a coven – a solitary witch has lots of power, but put together a few witches and they have so much more power combined.

Full moon circles don't have to be able casting spells or chanting or anything weird. A full moon circle might involve yoga, meditation, using crystals, journaling, or sharing your gratitude with others. I've been to full moon cacao ceremonies, full moon tea rituals & full moon yoga classes. Online, you'll find a range of live full moon events too, so you can join from the comfort of your home. I regularly hold online full moon events, such as live meditations, or full moon circles within the Herbal Moon Goddess Academy community, holding space for us all to connect with the power of the full moon.

There has never been so many options to join a full moon event so you can experience this full moon magic with others!

Moon Names

Have you noticed different full moons being called seemingly random names, like the Flower Moon, Blood Strawberry Moon, or Harvest Moon? These names are actually based on the traditional Native American or Colonial American names for the full moon in each month. These names can be interchangeable depending on the lunar cycle, but also to describe the climate in the local biosphere.

Here is a list of some traditional moon names, based on the Northern Hemisphere:

- **January**: Wolf Moon
- **February**: Snow Moon, Groundhog Moon, Eagle Moon or Bear Moon
- **March**: Worm Moon
- **April**: Pink Moon or Frog Moon.
- **May**: Flower Moon, Budding Moon, Frog Moon or Planting Moon
- **June**: Strawberry Moon
- **July**: Buck Moon
- **August**: Sturgeon Moon
- **September**: Corn Moon or Harvest Moon
- **October**: Hunter's Moon, Ice Moon
- **November**: Beaver Moon, Frost Moon
- **December**: Cold Moon, Snow Moon

But – what if you're in the Southern Hemisphere? Are these names the same? It's unlikely to be snowing in Australia during February, so the Snow Moon in February doesn't seem appropriate. As mentioned previously, the names of the full moons can be changed to reflect what's happening in your local climate. You may like to research the moon names given by your Indigenous people.

If you're in the Southern Hemisphere, you might like to use this list for more seasonally-appropriate moon names:

- **January**: Thunder Moon or Hay Moon
- **February**: Grain Moon, Corn Moon or Barley Moon

- **March**: Harvest Moon or Corn Moon
- **April**: Harvest Moon, Blood Moon or Hunter's Moon
- **May**: Hunter's Moon or Frost Moon
- **June**: Cold Moon or Long Night's Moon
- **July**: Ice Moon
- **August**: Snow Moon or Storm Moon
- **September**: Crow Moon, Worm Moon
- **October**: Seed Moon, Egg Moon, Fish Moon
- **November**: Flower Moon, Corn Moon
- **December**: Strawberry Moon, Rose Moon

But also keep in mind that you can name the moon whatever name you feel appropriate, according to what's happening in your local biosphere. For example, if a jacaranda tree in your front yard flowers every November, you may feel it appropriate to name the full moon in November the Jacaranda Moon. Observe what's going on in nature at that time of year, and make your moon manifesting practice UNIQUELY yours. Infuse your intention in your ceremonies as you slip into the flow & energy of nature.

Full moon journal prompts:
- Who or what do I need to forgive?
- What am I feeling grateful for?
- What am I celebrating or harvesting this full moon?
- What do I need to release & let go of?

Questions to ask your cards on the full moon:
- What energy is at its peak this full moon?

- What am I harvesting in my life this full moon?
- What do I need to release this full moon?
- Who do I need to forgive this full moon?

Action steps during the full moon:
- **Follow (or create) a ritual for gratitude, forgiveness & releasing.** Write out in your journal what you feel grateful for, who you need to forgive, and whatever you'd like to release. You may like to meditate on these feelings.

- **Charge your crystals, cards & other magickal tools.** Are your crystals not feeling as effective as they used to be? Maybe your tarot cards are out of sync? Leave them under the light of the full moon – for as long as you desire, whether that's an hour or all night.

- **Make moon water.** Moon water is also a fun way to capture the essence of the moon – leave a jar of water under the moonlight, and use this water for your house plants, or add to your rituals. If you used drinkable water, feel free to drink some moon water for an energy boost – just consume your moon water within 24 hours of making.

- **Join or host a full moon circle.** There's nothing quite like getting together with a group of like-minded witches for an evening of heightened energy & magick. Each moon circle I've ever joined or hosted has had a lasting effect on my life. There's a reason that covens are gaining popularity! Get together with your close friends for some fun with tarot or ceremonial cacao, or search for a full moon event in your local area.

- **Celebrate your successes**. The full moon is the best time of the cycle to see how far you've come over the past moon cycle, and celebrate your hard work. Reward yourself, say well done, and give yourself a pat on the back! Check in on your successes and acknowledge your progress towards your goals.

CHAPTER 4

Waning Moon

+ LET GO + REALIGN + REVIEW + SURRENDER +

*"But even when the moon looks like it's waning...it's
actually never changing shape.
Don't ever forget that."*
— *Ai Yazawa*

Let go of your goals and surrender to the Divine plan of the Universe. The waning moon is when we naturally feel into what needs to be released from our lives so we can realign with our true purpose. The overall theme of the waning moon is letting go. When we let go, we make space in our lives for new intentions to grow. Don't be afraid to let go!

From the time of the full moon until the new moon, the moon is waning. The moon will rise during the night hours, and set during the morning.

Like the waxing moon, we can break down the waning moon into different phases:
- Waning gibbous
- Last quarter moon
- Waning crescent
- Balsamic or dark moon.

Waning gibbous

+ SHARE + GIVE GENEROUSLY + REALIGN +

"With freedom, books, flowers, and the moon, who could not be happy?"
- Oscar Wilde

The waning gibbous marks the shift of the moon from full to beginning to wane. After the heightened energy of the full moon, we are still feeling energetic & very aware of our emotions & intuition. This is a great time for sharing your successes with others – we'll feel naturally communicative during this time of the lunar cycle.

During the waning gibbous phase, the moon rises later and later each night, until rising around midnight at the last quarter moon. You may catch a sight of the moon setting in the west in the mornings too.

There can be sleep disturbances with this heightened energy – you might find yourself tossing & turning in bed with ideas running through your mind, or ruminating over events that have been happening during this high-energy full moon period. If you're finding yourself with too much energy & mental activity in the evenings, try to work it off early in the day with exercise.

For entrepreneurs & business owners, launching a new offer during the full moon means that you'll feel energized to share it with your followers during the waning gibbous. You'll be feeling confident about your work, and confidence magnetizes paying customers. This can be a great opportunity when you naturally feel like making offers, working on your sales pages & promoting your work.

On the flip-side, the waning gibbous is not just about TAKING, but it is also about GIVING BACK. If you work on gratitude during the full moon, chances are that your heart is overflowing with kindness right now. How can you donate time or energy to a good cause? This is when we love to promote others, or when we perform random acts of kindness. Use your energy not only for your own needs, but to spread a bit of love + light to others too. We are all connected – we are all human, living this thing called life. It doesn't hurt to be kind & generous to others, especially when you see others who don't have such an abundant life as you do.

Realignment often comes up during the waning gibbous phase. After releasing during the climax of the moon's energy, we feel a shift as we realign with what we truly want to manifest. Your expectations, goals or ideas may come up for review, and adjustments are made. Perhaps you realize you were aiming too high and now you're going to lower your expectations. Maybe you've experienced so much success that you're raising your goals. The waning gibbous gives you an opportunity to reflect & make adjustments as needed.

This can be a great opportunity for editing your work. You've worked long hours during the waxing gibbous moon to achieve your goals & manifest your intentions, and you've celebrated the completion of these goals on the full moon. Now you can go over your work and fix any mistakes, or improve on your first draft.

Waning gibbous journal prompts:
- What am I excited to share with others?
- How can I be generous to others in my community?
- What needs to be adjusted or edited in my life?

Questions to ask your cards during the waning gibbous moon:
- What needs adjusting?
- Who do I need to give or be generous towards?
- What successes am I ready to share?

Action steps during the waning gibbous moon:
- **Perform a random act of kindness.** Pay it forward when you pay for your fuel, coffee or takeaway food. Help an elderly person. Donate your time or energy to a good cause. Open your heart and give generously – not only will you brighten someone else's day, but it will make you feel good too!

- **Check in with your intentions from the new moon or other goals that you've set.** Consider if anything needs adjusting or reviewing. Now is the time to refine your work and contemplate how to make it even better.

- **Share what you've been working on.** What are you feeling called to share with others? What has come into your life this full moon that you can share with others? Promote yourself and share your wisdom with others. Make an effort to share something – anything – with someone during the waning gibbous moon.

Last quarter

+ REVIEW + DECLUTTER + SIMPLIFY + CHANGE +

"If you don't like something, change it. If you can't change it, change your attitude."
– Maya Angelou

We'll often notice the last quarter moon in the sky during the morning hours as we look to the west. The last quarter moon rises around midnight, setting around midday. Seeing the moon as she descends towards the western horizon reminds me that it's time for turning my energy inwards.

The last quarter moon is often when we'll notice a real shift in our energy as we wind down from the intensity of the full moon. You'll begin to notice what you no longer have time, space or energy for in your life as you identify what you need to release & let go of – and then you'll do it.

Sometimes it might be something external to yourself that needs changing. Changes could be made to your work towards your goals, your working space, your home.

The energy of the last quarter moon prompts us to review & reflect on our lives. We consider what we need to edit out of our lives, to make space for something even better. This is a time for reviewing your goals, and contemplating what needs to change so your goals can manifest. Reflect on the progress of your goals. What could be improved? What can be removed?

You may find yourself proactively decluttering or cleaning your house, or perhaps you'll feel drawn to cleaning up other areas of your life, like your relationships, health or bad habits. Decluttering your physical space can have amazing effects on your emotions & energy too. Clutter in our homes or workspaces can block energy, or stagnate the energy of the entire area. Clearing this clutter literally frees up your energy. Have you noticed how a clean & tidy space has a fresher energy?

Often, we'll identify something else that we wish we could change, but it's not up to us to change. We might feel triggered by others or notice what we dislike about our lives. If it's not something you can physically change – try changing your mindset & feelings about it. The last quarter moon provides an opportunity for you to change – internally or externally. If something's not working out how you planned – can you change it? If not, can you change how you FEEL about it?

The last quarter moon is a time of simplifying our lives. What can you do to make life a bit easier over the next week? Work out the "bare minimum" of your commitments – the things that are absolutely necessary versus other things which could be rescheduled or cancelled. Stick to this bare minimum as much as you can during the next week so you can reserve your energy for introspection, healing & rest.

You may even like to use the last quarter moon to push yourself (just a little!) to schedule things in advance, prepare your meals & re-organize your commitments, so that you can actually take time off during the waning crescent moon. What would your future-self thank you for doing now?

Last quarter moon journal prompts:
- What is my "bare minimum" of commitments for the next week? Am I able to take time off work/study? Am I feeling over-committed with social events?
- What would my future-self thank me for doing now?
- What would I like to declutter from my life?

Questions to ask your cards during the last quarter moon:
- What do I need to declutter from my life?
- Why do I need to declutter this?

- How will I feel after decluttering this?

Action steps during the last quarter moon:
- **Declutter.** Identify areas in your home which are feeling a bit cluttered, and have fun decluttering! Free up some space and energy for something new to manifest into your life.

- **Release emotions and energetic blockages.** What emotions are you avoiding? What's been feeling heavy or stagnant lately? You may like to try meditation, sound bathing, chakra healing or yoga to shift your emotions & energy.

- **Review.** What could be simplified in your life? Review where you're spending your time and energy, and consider how you can edit your life to be more efficient. This step will help you immensely as we move into the energy of waning crescent moon phase.

Waning crescent

+ HEALING + INTROSPECTION + HIBERNATE +
+ SURRENDER +

"Go slowly, my lovely moon, go slowly."
— Khaled Hosseini

As the moon continues to wane, you'll notice you're feeling less energetic. Perhaps you'll feel a call to hibernate. Make regular time to reflect, journal & meditate. Turn inwards and reserve your energy. It's a time of introspection. Go slowly...

You'll see the waning crescent moon rising in the hours before dawn, and setting in the early afternoon.

If you're feeling overwhelmed, take this time to let go of some tasks from your to-do list. You might be putting too much pressure on yourself. What doesn't need to be attended to urgently? What can wait until you feel stronger? Go easy on yourself when the moon is in the waning crescent phase, allow yourself plenty of time to rest.

During the waning crescent moon, you may like to:

- Sleep more – go to bed earlier, or try a midday nap if you're feeling drained (just set your alarm so you don't nap for more than 30 minutes, or you could end up disrupting your sleep that night).

- Focus on self-care activities, like a relaxing bath, journaling, or watching a favourite movie.
- Journal out your thoughts – reflect on what you've achieved over these past few weeks, and what you'd like to change moving forward.
- Meditate more – quiet the mind and find inner peace & stillness.

Whatever you do during the waning crescent moon, just go easy on yourself. There's absolutely no need to keep pushing yourself if your energy is low.
This is probably my favourite thing about moon manifesting – the fact that it gives us permission to slow down and literally do nothing! I'm a lover of lazy manifesting – anything that helps me achieve my goals in a chilled, laidback way.

Even though it can feel counter-intuitive to just lay back, relax and wait for your goals to manifest, don't skip this step! Don't be tempted to just keep pushing yourself so you can achieve your goals faster. Most of the time, this leads to burnout & exhaustion. You'll usually be forced to take a break from your work anyway, because this exhaustion often leads to illness. In the months when I've been too busy with my work to actually take time off during the waning crescent, I've often ended up catching a cold or being bedridden with a killer migraine. Learn from my mistakes and save yourself the pain & inconvenience of illness!

I now know that it's important to take regular time off, and the waning crescent moon is the best opportunity to do it.

An interesting thing that happens when we take time off from our manifesting efforts. It's often during the times when we don't show up, or we focus our energy elsewhere, that our goals seem to manifest themselves. I've heard from so many women who manifested money while they were on vacation, or while they were asleep, or after they decided to have a social media detox. Remember, the Universe will work with you to co-create your goals! Don't feel guilty about relaxing and focusing your energy on caring for yourself. Chances are that your goals will start to manifest by themselves anyway. Indulge in your self-care!

Waning crescent journal prompts:
- How can I be more compassionate to myself today?
- If I could relax and do ANYTHING, what would I do?
- What tasks on my to-do list can wait until later? What tasks can I completely let go of?

Questions to ask your cards during the waning crescent moon:
- What can I let go of this week?
- What should I focus on healing?
- What will help me find inner stillness?

Action steps during the waning crescent moon:
- **Meditate.** Conserve your energy and spend time in silence. Take deep breaths as you switch off from the outside world. Listen to a guided meditation or relaxing music to help you focus on your inner realms. Come to stillness during this time of darkness.

- **Healing.** Make time & space for healing during the waning crescent moon. Journaling, yoga or energy healing can be super helpful during this moon phase, but going to bed early can be just as healing. Get plenty of rest & look after yourself lovingly.

Dark moon

+ STILLNESS + MEDITATION + HEALING +

"Everyone is a moon, and has a dark side which he never shows to anybody."
– Mark Twain

The dark moon, also known as the balsamic moon, occurs during the 1-2 days before the new moon, when the moon isn't visible in the sky (or perhaps you may get a glimpse of the moon just before sunrise, as the moon will rise about an hour before the sun).

The dark moon period is a time of finding stillness. Take time to meditate, attend a yin or restorative yoga class, journal & quietly reflect. This can be a beautiful time for healing, as you introspect & withdraw from the world around you.

This dark moon energy continues the theme of the waning crescent moon. It's so important to relax, let go of your burdens & focus on your own needs when the moon is in the last days of the cycle.

During this time, honour your energy levels. Collectively we can have quite low energy levels during the waning crescent & dark moon – marking the point in the moon cycle when our physical energy levels are at their lowest. Avoid overcommitting to social engagements or appointments, so you can have some much-needed quiet time.

I often get great ideas for beautiful healing rituals to do during the dark moon, such as setting up my yoga mat and following along with an online yin yoga class, followed by crystal healing, sound healing, and all sorts of other healing activities. But truthfully, often by the time of the dark moon, I've run out of energy and end up just chilling in front of the TV.

Healing is your own journey, so trust that you receive the right healing, in the right dosage, at the right time. Sometimes the Universe will give you opportunities to heal with yoga, and sometimes the Universe will give you opportunities to heal with a tub of Ben & Jerry's Dairy-free Seven Layer Coconut Bar ice cream. Healing can take many shapes & forms, so just make some space for healing during the dark moon – in whatever form feels best for you.

The dark moon is a potent time for shadow work. Bringing your inner feelings to light so they can be transformed is a powerful practice. You can use the dark moon energy to banish stuff from your life – try releasing & banishing addictions, negative thought patterns or relationship difficulties. This time of the lunar cycle is perfect for doing shadow work, because it frees up your energy & emotions just in time for a new lunar cycle to begin. There's nothing better than having a clean slate to work with on the new moon.

Dark moon journal prompts:
- What do I need to heal?
- What will bring me the most healing right now?
- How can I rest & recharge fully during this time?

Questions to ask your cards during the dark moon:
- What needs healing now?
- What needs to be banished from my life?
- What is the most effective thing for me to do during the dark moon?

Action steps during the dark moon:
- **Rest.** Allow yourself some extra time for sleeping (or at least, resting). Reserve your energy, take things off your to-do list. It's okay to stop for a while and just rest & recharge.

- **Self-care.** What can you do to fill your cup? If you must do something during the dark moon, let it be focused on yourself. Pamper yourself, nourish yourself, renew yourself. The dark moon is a wonderful time for relaxing in a warm bath, going to bed early to meditate, or moving through a slow yin yoga session (try an online class so you don't have to leave home – or even get out of your pyjamas!).

- **Heal.** Is there something coming up for healing in your life? Make space for healing to occur during this moon phase. It could be as simple as getting more sleep or rest, or maybe you feel the need for crystal healing, reiki, massage, or consumable medicine like supplements or herbal medicines. Be gentle to yourself as you invite healing to occur in your life.

Black moon

+ MANIFESTING + AMPLIFICATION +
+ TRANSFORMATION +

"There are nights when the wolves are silent and only the moon howls."
- George Carlin

Black moons are a rare event, rather than part of the regular moon cycle, but a book on moon manifesting could not be complete without mentioning the power of black or blue moons!

Black moons can be defined as:
- The second new moon in a calendar month.
- The third new moon of four new moons in a tropical season (usually there are only 3 new

moons in a season – this event occurs roughly every 3 years).
- Or, as the second new moon in the same zodiac sign.

It's generally considered to only be astrologically significant when using the latter definition – a black moon being the second consecutive new moon in the same zodiac sign (but you can absolutely use any definition you prefer!). For this second consecutive new moon to occur in the same zodiac sign, the first new moon will fall within the first or second degree of the zodiac sign (between 0-2 degrees), and the second new moon will fall in the 29th degree.

Dates of the next black moons

20 April 2023: Black Moon in Aries
21 September 2025: Black Moon (and Solar Eclipse) in Virgo
21/22 July 2028: Black Moon (and Solar Eclipse) in Cancer
19 June 2031: Black Moon in Gemini

Many astrologers agree that the degrees of 0 and 29 are critical, in terms of Western astrology. Any planets in the very first or last degree of a zodiac sign can trigger crises, transformation and soul growth. There are karmic ties related to planets falling in the first or last degree of a sign. A black moon will always fall in this critical 29th degree (and sometimes the preceding new moon will fall in the critical 1st degree also). This is why the energy of these black moons can be very potent – they lay the foundations for great change & transformation to occur.

The first new moon before a black moon occurs is a time of beginnings. Enthusiasm & powerful new beginnings are associated with this new moon energy. We may act on impulse when setting intentions for this new moon.

Then, approximately 29 days later, the black moon falls in the same sign in the 29th degree. This second new moon in this cycle brings an opportunity to review & refine your intentions from the previous new moon. This opportunity helps you increase your manifesting powers as you get clearer & more confident about what you want to ask from the Universe.

Use this black moon manifesting magic by setting strong intentions. Your intentions will be amplified, and the Universe will start to shift things so your intentions will be manifested. Be mindful of what you wish for!

Be prepared for changes & transformation when working with the power of the black moon. Growth isn't always easy. Sometimes we set intentions & ask the Universe to provide something for us – but then we're not prepared to do the work, or we're not prepared for everything else that comes with those intentions.

Black moons help us identify where work & aligned action is needed. The intentions we set on the prior new moon may not have to be totally aligned with our core desires because we rushed in too fast or didn't think things through. The black moon gives us a chance to try again, because now we KNOW what we actually want to manifest, and what we need to do to make it happen. We've thought about the consequences of our wishes, and we're prepared to do what it takes.

Blue moon

+ REBIRTH + SOUL GROWTH +
+ TRANSFORMATION +

"Once in a blue moon, someone like you comes along."
– Van Morrison

Blue moons can be defined in a number of ways, similarly to black moons:

1. As the second full moon in a calendar month.
2. As the third of four full moons in a tropical season.
3. Or, as the second full moon in the same zodiac sign.

Just like black moons, I've found it to be mostly significant when the blue moon is defined as the second full moon in the same zodiac sign. Similarly to black moons, blue moons will fall in the critical 29th degree of the zodiac sign. This critical degree can be associated with crises, completion, fate and soul growth – which can explain why blue moons can feel intense!

This second full moon in a zodiac sign gives a powerful boost to whatever you're manifesting for that moon cycle. Full moons are a time of harvesting the seeds we sow at the new moon, so a blue moon is a bonus second harvest! The energy of the full moon is amplified during a blue moon. Expect the energy to be intense, especially if you have any planets around 29 degrees in your natal chart.

This intensity can cause rapid transformation & change in our lives. A heated argument. A sudden impulse. A Divine download of inspiration. Blue moons can push you out of your comfort zone, but trust that this push is driving you down the right path.

Use blue moons to your manifesting advantage by knowing in advance when a blue moon is going to occur. I've listed the next blue moons for your reference.

Dates of the next blue moons

21 July 2024: Blue Moon in Capricorn
22 September 2029: Blue Moon in Pisces
21 August 2032: Blue Moon in Aquarius

As you can see, blue moons occur rather infrequently, so you don't want to miss the rare opportunity to manifest with the power of the blue moon!

You'll need to set intentions on the NEW moon corresponding with that blue moon – for example, set your intentions on the 11th January 2024 during the new moon in Capricorn to manifest these intentions intensely with the blue moon in Capricorn on the 21st July 2024.

However, if you miss that window of opportunity to set intentions 6 months before the blue moon, don't worry! You'll find that the Universe will naturally push you towards intense transformation on the blue moon anyway. Direct your energy towards the changes that you want to create in your life, and let the blue moon energy make this magic for you.

I feel that moon manifesting is all about learning how to work in alignment with the energies of the moon. Otherwise, things can get chaotic & out of our control – especially on full moons, blue moons, or eclipses.

CHAPTER 5

The Moon Through The Zodiac

Now that you have an understanding of the different moon phases and how to work with each phase, we're going to take it to the next level. In this chapter, you'll discover the energy of each of the 12 zodiac signs, plus how to combine the energy of the moon phase with the zodiac sign.

It doesn't matter what your sun sign is – we ALL feel the energy of the moon throughout the entire zodiac.

The 12 zodiac signs are:

- **Aries**. New beginnings & following your passions.
- **Taurus**. Creating practical plans to manifest your deepest desires.

- **Gemini**. Networking & communicating with others.
- **Cancer**. Creating security in your life.
- **Leo**. Shining bright to be a beacon of inspiration.
- **Virgo**. Being of service to others.
- **Libra**. Giving & receiving support.
- **Scorpio**. Transforming your inner emotions.
- **Sagittarius**. Finding a deeper meaning to life.
- **Capricorn**. Strategizing to achieve your long-term goals.
- **Aquarius**. Tweaking & adjusting plans.
- **Pisces**. Renewing your emotions & energy.

Aries

+ ACTION + COURAGE + AMBITION +

Aries is the first sign of the zodiac, symbolizing new beginnings, individuality, ambitions, and authenticity. Ruled by fire and Mars, the Aries energy is all about taking action & following your passions.

As the first sign in the zodiac, the Aries energy helps us find our identity & to be confident in who we are. Find your individuality – you don't always need to blend in with the crowd.

Take ambitious action. Feel confident & courage to take the next step. The moon in Aries will get you fired up towards your goals! Be wary that the moon in Aries can also provoke fiery emotions, like anger and impatience. Remember that even though you have your own ambitious goals to strive for, be thoughtful & courteous of others. Calm your temper. Don't be frustrated if others aren't moving at your fast pace.

The moon in Aries can spark your creativity. We'll often feel more confident to express ourselves with authenticity, adding our original flair to projects & pursuing what we are personally interested in.

♈

Aries correspondences

Ruling planet: Mars
Element: Fire
Crystals: carnelian, citrine, diamond, bloodstone, red jasper, sardonyx
Herbs: cayenne, chilli, nettle, garlic, mustard, cumin, honeysuckle
Essential oils: black pepper
Body parts: head, face, teeth
Chakras: solar plexus
Tarot: IV The Emperor

New moon in Aries: Start new creative projects. Get inspired with a creative vision board. Create a new beginning in your life.

Waxing moon in Aries: Take courageous action towards your goals. Don't let anything stop you from achieving your goals. Take initiative & make the first move. Follow your original plans. Feel confident.

Full moon in Aries: Celebrate your ambitious achievements. Creative projects are coming to a peak or completion. Be grateful for the things that make you unique. Do something fun & empowering to celebrate the full moon.

Waning moon in Aries: Be ambitious & proactive about taking time off to rest. Let go of anger, frustration & impatience. Review your ideas. Reflect on your creative projects. Share your passions with others. Receive a relaxing head massage.

Taurus

+ BEAUTY + NATURE + GROUNDING +
+ PRACTICALITY +

Taurus, ruled by Venus and the element of earth, is a sign of practicality, luxury & beauty. When the moon is in Taurus, we feel called to slow down & focus on our own self-care. You may decide to book in for beauty treatments at this time or spend extra time & energy on your beauty or self-care rituals. Our senses are ignited with the moon in Taurus, so indulge in sensual delights such as scented candles, delicious treats or aromatherapy.

As an earth sign, Taurus encourages us to ground ourselves and connect with nature. Spend time outdoors, tend to the garden or go for a nature walk. Sit amongst trees & flowers, perhaps taking the opportunity to meditate or do yoga.

When the moon moves through Taurus, we'll often feel called to slow down. How can you turn your original ideas into a sustainable project? Work out the practicalities during this time and ground your ideas into reality.

Taurus helps you focus on your core values & desires. What do you TRULY want to manifest in your life? With the serene, calming energy of Taurus, we can tune into our inner self to discover what we deeply desire to manifest in our realities.

♉

Taurus correspondences:

Ruling planet: Venus
Element: Earth
Crystals: rose quartz, jade, aquamarine, emerald, kunzite, malachite, rhodonite, lapis lazuli, kyanite, diamond, tiger's eye, selenite, tourmaline, chrysoprase
Herbs: rose, sage, mint, violet, dandelion, foxglove, slippery elm, tansy, thyme, licorice, lovage, goldenrod, myrtle, fenugreek
Essential oils: rose
Body parts: throat, neck, thyroid
Chakras: heart
Tarot: V The Hierophant

New moon in Taurus: Set practical goals & intentions. Connect with nature & ground yourself. Plant new seeds – literally & figuratively. Find inspiration from nature. Manifest abundance. Dream of your money goals or the physical things you want to manifest, like a new house, car, jewellery, etc.

Waxing moon in Taurus: Take practical action towards manifesting your goals. Grow your abundance. Focus on making money. Take aligned action towards manifesting your deepest desires. Focus on sustainability & practicality.

Full moon in Taurus: Celebrate the abundance you've received. Show gratitude for the money & possessions in your life. Indulge in luxuries.

Waning moon in Taurus: Focus on self-care. Spend time relaxing outdoors. Weed the garden. Relax your body — try yin yoga or a long meditation. Clear energetic blockages in the throat & heart chakras. Heal the throat, neck or thyroid.

Gemini

Gemini, ruled by air and Mercury, is the sign of communication & networking. The moon in Gemini encourages connecting with others, quick-thinking, finding inspiration & collaborating with others. When the moon is in Gemini, you might feel more confident to express your ideas.

Ask yourself: who can help me achieve my goals quicker? The Gemini energy is about finding strengths in a partnership to create an even stronger team. Who could you ask for advice? Who could you add to your team? Who can teach you what you need to know?

Find inspiration through reading, reading posts online or chatting with others. Follow whatever sparks your curiosity! Keep an open mind – a fresh perspective could give you deeper insights.

If there's something that needs swift action, the moon in Gemini might be the time to tackle it. The Gemini energy encourages fast action – use this energy to put your ideas into action.

Important writing or speaking projects are suited to the Gemini energy. Use this time to schedule social media posts, blog posts or newsletters. Write those important emails, scripts or sales copy now. Work on your next book. Head out to a networking event.

Your communication skills will be heightened, and you'll find it easier to express your ideas.

The shadow side of the Gemini energy is feeling easily distracted & procrastinating. Try making a to-do list in the morning, so you stay focused & on-task during the day. If you're getting easily distracted, try grounding yourself through meditation, yoga or pranayama. Regularly stop and take a few deep breaths – it will help!

♊

Gemini correspondences

Ruling planet: Mercury
Element: Air
Crystals: agate, aquamarine, black tourmaline, tourmalinated quartz, rutilated quartz, clear quartz, chrysocolla, citrine, serpentine, tiger's eye, fluorite, larimar, onyx, jade, apophyllite
Herbs: mullein, horehound, hyssop, lavender, mint, fern, yarrow, meadowsweet, skullcap, parsley, lemon balm, elecampane, coltsfoot, marjoram, caraway, lobelia, tansy, aniseed, southernwood, lily of the valley, mace, filbert, goat's rue, almond, bracken, dill, aniseed
Essential oils: orange bergamot, fennel, lavender, lemongrass, peppermint, marjoram, oregano, geranium

Body parts: nervous system, brain, mouth, throat, lungs, hands, arms, thymus
Chakras: throat
Tarot: VI The Lovers

New moon in Gemini: Focus on your intentions. Journal your ideas. Be open to inspirational downloads & insights from the Universe. Start a reading a new book. Begin studying. Make an essential oil blend to diffuse during the moon cycle ahead – choose essential oils which support your new moon intentions.

Waxing moon in Gemini: Multitask to get things done. Take quick action. Follow your curiosity. Be confident & speak up. Connect & collaborate with someone to help you reach your goals faster. Write a to-do list so you can stay focused.

Full moon in Gemini: Share your story with the world. Celebrate with friends. Party! Journal about your recent achievements. Feel grateful for the support in your life. Launch a book, online course or workshop.

Waning moon in Gemini: Release social commitments. Banish gossip. Find stillness in the chaos. Let go of overwhelm. Do yoga to still the mind. Remove tasks from your to-do list. Relax your shoulders & arms. Release anxiety, depression or other mental health issues.

Cancer

+ EMOTIONS + HOME + FAMILY + SECURITY +

Cancer, ruled by the Moon and water, is a highly sensitive & emotional sign. Our emotions & intuition are often heightened with the moon in Cancer – you may pick up on subtle energetic clues, or feel empathic & be able to read other's feelings more easily.

With the moon in Cancer, it's an ideal time to work on your emotions & create a sense of emotional security. What fears have been coming up for you? What negative emotions or feelings are you holding onto? The Cancer energy helps you become aware of these feelings, so you can work through them & find release. How would you like to feel INSTEAD of feeling scared, fearful, sad, angry, resentful, guilty or ashamed?

With your intuition heightened at this time, you can trust your intuitive abilities. Listen to those gut feelings – even if it doesn't seem logical, or you don't know why – just trust those instincts.

As Cancer is ruled by water, including the water element in your rituals can help you connect with this Cancer energy. Try including things like a bath, herbal tea, swimming, or fresh flowers in a vase.

Working with crystals and herbal teas can provide emotional support with the moon in Cancer. Charge a crystal with a positive affirmation to help you transform your emotions. Create a mindful herbal tea blend to support your wellbeing. Infuse your intentions into your tea & crystals. This mindful practice will help you tune into the sensitivity of Cancer.

The Cancer energy is associated with our home & family life. What can you add to or remove from your home to enhance your comfort levels? How can you nurture your family or the people you care about? How can you create more security & stability in your life? With the Cancer energy closely associated to motherhood & pregnancy, this can be an ideal time for womb healing or ancestral healing.

Along those lines of security & stability, Cancer is also associated with financial security. The moon in Cancer can bring up your financial insecurities, providing an opportunity for you to consider how you can create regular & consistent income. What actions do you need to take to ensure income security? How can you feel more financially secure? Where is your money being spent, and where is your money coming from?

♋

Cancer correspondences

Ruling planet: Moon
Element: Water
Crystals: moonstone, calcite, chalcedony, pearl, amber, emerald, cat's eye, carnelian, rhodonite, opal, pink tourmaline, moss agate, dendritic agate, fire agate, chrysoprase, ruby, turquoise

Herbs: lemon balm, iris, water lily, lotus, jasmine, hyssop, borage, passionflower, moonwort, poppy, lemon, tarragon, eucalyptus, mint, verbena, willow, marigold, chickweed, honeysuckle
Essential oils: lemon, chamomile, clary sage, rosemary, lemon balm, peppermint, eucalyptus
Body parts: breasts, stomach, female reproductive organs
Chakras: third eye
Tarot: VII The Chariot

New moon in Cancer: Set intentions to do with your home or family life. Plan how to create financial security. Meditate & find emotional security. Focus on FEELING good.

Waxing moon in Cancer: Charge a crystal with an affirmation. Take action based on your intuition & feelings. Honour your emotions, and do what you FEEL like doing instead of what you SHOULD be doing. Infuse your morning coffee or tea with your intentions for the day.

Full moon in Cancer: Release emotions which don't feel good. Have a bath ritual – add crystals, herbs, essential oils or other luxurious bath additions. Celebrate with family – make a delicious meal to share or do something your family loves to do together. Feel grateful for the security & safety in your life.

Waning moon in Cancer: Let go of past trauma. Relax in the comfort of your home. Share intuitive insights with others. Read your tarot cards or horoscope. Receive spiritual healing. Work on ancestral or womb healing.

Leo

+ MOTIVATION + LEADERSHIP + CREATIVITY +

Leo, ruled by fire and the Sun, symbolizes creativity, fun & play. With the moon in Leo, we can feel inspired & motivated to shine to our true potential. This fun & ambitious energy provides a good dose of confidence & courage, helping us to overcome our fears.

Be original & authentic as you make progress towards creative projects. Add your own original flair to whatever you're working on. Channel your creativity into your daily tasks – maybe get out some coloured pencils or stickers, or add some emojis to online messages.

You can take your creativity further when the moon is in Leo and dedicate some time to painting, drawing, sculpting, or making music. What lights your creative fire? If you're not sure what to do, channel your inner child. Imagine you are the 4 year old version of yourself – would you want to make a big messy fingerpainting? Or maybe you'd want to play the piano & sing along? Follow what your inner child is calling you to do! It's important that we find regular time to drop our guards so we can have fun and just PLAY. When was the last time you made time for play?

The moon in Leo can prompt us to step up into a leadership position. We feel more confident in our ability to lead, make decisions, and to motivate others. What do you need to take control of in your life? Perhaps you need to step up and be an effective leader in a group situation, in your family, or among colleagues. Or perhaps you just need to realise that you are your OWN leader, and if you want your goals to manifest then it's up to YOU to make it happen.

Work with the element of fire when the moon is in Leo. Add candles, wands, or burn things. Seriously – burning letters filled with hurt & anger can be very therapeutic! Of course, always consider safety – you can burn paper over a fireproof vessel (like a ceramic bowl or metal cauldron), or throw your letter into a fireplace.

What would you do if you KNEW you could not fail? The moon in Leo reminds us that we are supported by the Universe. What would you do if you knew you had unlimited support towards whatever goal you aim for? Use the Leo confidence to show up courageously & fearlessly.

♌

Leo correspondences

Ruling planet: Sun
Element: Fire
Crystals: sunstone, citrine, pyrite, amber, tiger's eye, carnelian, ruby, diamond, yellow calcite, cat's eye, garnet, quartz, smoky quartz, hematite, kunzite, topaz

Herbs: sunflower, chamomile, calendula, marigold, bay leaves, frankincense, calamus, hops, mistletoe, citrus, fennel, eyebright, saffron, rosemary, St John's wort, daffodil
Essential oils: neroli, orange, fennel, frankincense, rosemary
Body parts: hair, spine, heart, blood, lungs
Chakras: third eye, crown
Tarot: VIII Strength

New moon in Leo: Set intentions to be more confident, courageous, inspirational, or to overcome fears. Start new creative projects. Intend to become famous. Connect with your inner child. Plan more time for fun, games & play. Find inspiration from within.

Waxing moon in Leo: Take inspired action. Find inspiration from others – read inspirational books or quotes, or get a pep talk from a friend. Be ambitious towards your goals. Overcome your fears & resistance so you can take the next step. Follow your inner child & play. Stay optimistic & have faith in your goals.

Full moon in Leo: Bring creative projects to completion. Share your creative endeavours with others. Perform & show off your skills. Play, laugh, and have fun – remember you don't have to be serious all the time.

Waning moon in Leo: Use creativity as a form of self-care. Reflect & refine your skills. Review your creative projects – what could be improved, or what's working well? Let go & forgive wounds from your childhood. Heal the inner child.

Virgo

+ HEALTH + DAILY ROUTINES + PRODUCTIVITY +

Virgo, an earth sign ruled by Mercury, symbolizes health, routines & daily work. With the moon in Virgo, our attention goes towards perfecting the little details. We feel productive towards our goals, and we use routine to help us make steady progress.

The moon in Virgo can be a helpful time for planning ahead, creating a routine or habit, focusing on health & fitness goals, and finding more efficient ways of completing tasks.

Spend this time working on written projects, looking after your finances, detoxing, exercising, and scheduling ahead. It's a good time to plan ahead to ensure you meet your goals – you might feel like planning out + preparing healthy meals for the week ahead so you can meet your health goals, or planning your budget in alignment with your financial goals.

As an earth sign, with the moon in Virgo we'll feel called to focus on the practical aspects of our lives. Our physical health & the physical work we do can become a focal point. How could you improve your health? How can you organize your day more efficiently? How can you be of greater service, to yourself & to the rest of the world?

Incorporate the element of earth into your Virgo moon rituals by spending time in nature, working in your garden, and by grounding yourself. Regular meditation & choosing healthy, nourishing meals will help you feel good during this time.

$$\text{♍}$$

Virgo correspondences

Ruling planet: Mercury
Element: Earth
Crystals: agate, fluorite, peridot, sardonyx, jade, amazonite, citrine, garnet, moonstone, sodalite, opal, amber, carnelian, aquamarine
Herbs: cornflower, fennel, skullcap, valerian, plantain, elder, lavender, morning glory, narcissus, rosemary, root vegetables, grains
Essential oils: lavender, chamomile, thyme, fennel, rosemary
Body parts: abdomen, intestines, spine
Chakras: throat
Tarot: IX The Hermit

New moon in Virgo: Set new health goals. Start a new job. Create a fitness routine. Plant seeds in the garden. Meditate outdoors. Plant seeds in the garden.

Waxing moon in Virgo: Take action towards your health goals. Write a to-do list – then do everything on the list. Find ways to be more productive. Plan ahead, focusing on the small details. Commit to exercising regularly and eating nourishing foods.

Full moon in Virgo: Celebrate your health successes. Cook a nourishing feast to celebrate. Harvest the results of your projects from recent months. Show gratitude for the abundance & prosperity in your life. Open your heart chakra – try a ceremony with yoga, meditation, crystals and/or cacao.

Waning moon in Virgo: Review your health goals, diet or exercise regime. Declutter your home & workspace. Reorganize your cupboards. Edit your life, removing what no longer feels aligned. Weed your garden.

Libra

+ ROMANCE + SUPPORT + RELATIONSHIPS +

Libra, ruled by Venus and air, is the sign of romance, relationships & support. Self-care rituals are a favourable activity when the moon is in Libra. Indulge in pampering yourself. Make a homemade face mask, soak your feet in a footbath, give your hair a moisturizing treatment. If you have a partner, include them too! Add some chocolate, wine & roses to make it extra romantic.

Relationships are a focus of the Libra energy. Pay attention to those you are close with. Which relationships are thriving, and which relationships are fading? Who have you been neglecting? Work on improving your relationships. It could start with phoning a family member, or sending a text to a good friend.

The Libra energy helps us find more peace in our lives. How can you bring more calming energy into your life? How can you find more harmony? This harmonious energy helps us feel more aligned with our goals.

The moon in Libra is a time for finding & giving support. Where do you need more support in your life? How can you support those around you? If you need help, now is the time to reach out and ask for it.

However, the biggest form of support we can give ourselves is through self-love. The moon in Libra can be a good time for repeating self-love affirmations, or tapping (If you've never tried, research EFT or

76

emotional freedom technique. It's literally life-changing!).

When we love ourselves deeply, we release the need for external validation. We can be our own biggest cheerleader!

Use the element of air when working with this Libra energy. You can play music, diffuse essential oils, smoke cleanse your home, meditate, or repeat mantras to bring more peace, harmony & loving vibes into your life.

$$\underline{\Omega}$$

Libra correspondences

Ruling planet: Venus
Element: Air
Crystals: rose quartz, jade, lapis lazuli, morganite, opal, bloodstone, ametrine, lepidolite, kunzite, moonstone, peridot, sapphire, sunstone, aventurine, aquamarine
Herbs: juniper, thyme, catnip, bearberry, clivers, angelica, violets, mallow, parsley, pansy, feverfew, burdock, butterfly pea
Essential oils: juniper, rose, jasmine, orange, peppermint, thyme
Body parts: kidneys, lower back
Chakras: heart
Tarot: XI Justice

New moon in Libra: Set new intentions for your relationships. Start a mentorship, relationship or partnership. Begin a self-care routine. Plan to bring more romance into your life. Set intentions to follow your artistic or musical passions. Get a new haircut, or freshen up your wardrobe.

Waxing moon in Libra: Buy yourself fresh flowers. Talk with a mentor, friend, or someone you trust. Repeat self-love affirmations such as "I love myself deeply & completely". Ask for advice. Spend time creating romance & beauty.

Full moon in Libra: Celebrate with a romantic candlelit dinner. Enjoy a luxurious bath (add bubble bath, bath salts, essential oils, flowers, or whatever else you desire). Feel grateful for the support in your life. Send notes of gratitude to the people you appreciate. Perform a beauty ritual or self-care ritual. Open your heart chakra through forgiveness, compassion & gratitude.

Waning moon in Libra: Reflect on your relationships. Spend extra time on self-care or beauty. Let go of the need for external validation. Reach out for support if you need it. Support others however you can. Put your own needs first.

Scorpio

+ TRANSFORMATION + PSYCHIC POWERS + + FINANCES +

Scorpio, ruled by water and Pluto, is a sign of transformation & rebirth. We can feel more intuitive & emotional with the moon in Scorpio. These heightened emotions make the Scorpio moon a good time for shadow work. Move through your fears & insecurities, transforming them into confidence & positivity.

Our psychic powers can be heightened while the moon is transiting Scorpio. Trust your subconscious nudges, follow your inner compass. Your instincts are leading you in the right direction. Explore your psychic abilities through reading your own tarot or oracle cards, or explore your horoscope. Listen to your intuition as you receive this guidance from the Universe.

Transformation is the overall theme of the Scorpio energy. Transforming your emotions, energy vibrations or even relationships becomes easier with the moon in fluid Scorpio. Embrace change and acknowledge what needs to be released from your life. What are you holding onto which no longer feels good? Let go what's no longer aligned so you can make room for something better to grow.

Scorpio is associated with business & finances, so the moon in Scorpio can be a good time to review our financial situation & to manifest more money. Work on your business plans, review your investments & focus on how you can grow your finances. Money mindset work is highly aligned with the Scorpio energy!

Incorporate water into your Scorpio moon rituals to connect with this water sign. Visit a river, lake or ocean. Stay hydrated with your favourite herbal tea. Have a long soak in the bath. Make a crystal essence.

♏

Scorpio correspondences

Ruling planet: Pluto
Element: Water
Crystals: garnet, smoky quartz, bloodstone, labradorite, obsidian, sardonyx, malachite, moonstone, kunzite, rhodochrosite, ruby, emerald, boji stone, lodestone, moldavite, apache tear obsidian, charoite
Herbs: red raspberry leaf, lady's mantle, peony, cramp bark, damiana, jasmine, cohosh, milk thistle, squaw vine, horehound, sarsaparilla, aloe vera, gentian, wormwood, ginseng, cascara, dong quai
Essential oils: patchouli, jasmine, rose
Body parts: reproductive organs, genitals
Chakras: solar plexus, sacral
Tarot: XIII Death

New moon in Scorpio: Set intentions for your business or finances. Start new financial goals. Begin an EFT tapping ritual. Consider how your vibration & energy affects your physical world. Consult your tarot cards or horoscope before setting goals & intentions.

Waxing moon in Scorpio: Manifest money FAST. Transform fear into confidence. Feel the fear but do it anyway. Repeat abundance affirmations. Change how you're feeling. Transform your energy, transform your life. Take intuition action towards your goals. Follow your instincts.

Full moon in Scorpio: Release your fears. Do shadow work. Transform your emotions. Let go of emotional insecurity & jealousy. Receive financial prosperity & abundance into your life. Practice divination, like tarot reading, scrying or palm reading.

Waning moon in Scorpio: Let go of your insecurities. Do a cord cutting ritual. Work on healing your chakras, especially the solar plexus & sacral chakras. Receive an energy healing. Release debts. Feel into the energy of a situation before making decisions. Receive spiritual guidance or advice from a psychic, reader or healer.

Sagittarius

+ EXPANSION + EXPLORATION + EDUCATION +
+ DEEP MEANING +

Sagittarius is ruled by Jupiter and fire. With the moon in Sagittarius, we feel like going deep into our passions. We study, we create, we read. We feel more adventurous, yearning for traveling. We may immerse ourselves in other cultures by eating exotic cuisines or practicing a foreign language.

Explore different ethnicities while the moon is in Sagittarius. You'll find emotional satisfaction through eating exotic cuisines or conversing in a foreign tongue. Spice things up with your food, and you'll spice up your creativity too.

Connect with the fire element of Sagittarius through including candles, fire or wands in your rituals. Warming herbs such as chilli, cinnamon & ginger will ignite your curiosity & passion.

What are your goals, and what do you need to learn about to help you manifest them? What knowledge will help you most right now? The moon in Sagittarius highlights what area of your life you naturally crave more information about. What do you love to deeply explore?

The Sagittarius energy is about going DEEP so you can find more meaning & magic in your life. Don't just skim the surface – keeping asking yourself WHY, keeping going deeper, exploring new ideas and expanding your mind.

This can be why spirituality, religion & faith seem to come to the surface when the moon is transiting Sagittarius. Having that faith in something higher can help us find more meaning & purpose to our everyday actions. How do you goals fit in with this deeper meaning or purpose to your life? Explore your spiritual or philosophical views when the moon is in Sagittarius.

♐

Sagittarius correspondences

Ruling planet: Jupiter
Element: Fire
Crystals: lapis lazuli, sodalite, turquoise, aventurine, smoky quartz, malachite, labradorite, pink tourmaline, snowflake obsidian, azurite, sugilite, chalcedony, garnet, ruby, charoite, blue lace agate
Herbs: bay, hops, agrimony, dandelion, calendula, sage, anise, red clover, wood betony, borage, burdock, mallow, feverfew, horsetail, narcissus, goldenrod, carnation
Essential oils: sandalwood, frankincense, myrrh, sage
Body parts: hips, thighs
Chakras: sacral
Tarot: XIV Temperance

New moon in Sagittarius: Set new intentions for books to read or places to travel. Plan your travel bucket list.

Set goals for learning a new language. Find inspiration from foreign cultures. Begin studying. Begin teaching. Begin writing a book.

Waxing moon in Sagittarius: Listen to & act on your mentor's advice. Turn to spirituality for inspiration & motivation. Have faith in your Higher Purpose. Expand your horizons. Learn about something to help you reach your goals this week. Teach others about your passions.

Full moon in Sagittarius: Release anything unaligned with the deeper meaning of your life. Release restrictions holding you back from freedom. Let go of "knowing it all". Do a hip-releasing yoga flow. Perform a fire releasing ritual. Let go of your frustrations with others. Celebrate by travelling or going on vacation. Be grateful for the knowledge of others.

Waning moon in Sagittarius: Review what you've learnt over the past few weeks. Relax with a creative project. Read for pleasure. Reflect on your academic achievements & goals. Connect with your spiritual practices, religion or faith.

Capricorn

+ STRATEGY + CONTROL + SELF-DISCIPLINE +
+ CAREER +

Capricorn is ruled by Saturn and the element of earth. The moon in Capricorn helps us focus on our long-term goals in a practical sense. We strategize & we move forward. We find the self-discipline to keep taking action towards our long-term goals, knowing that we may not reap the rewards for a long time.

Connect with the Earth element of Capricorn through spending time in nature. Walk in a forest or a park. Pick fresh flowers. Water your houseplants. Grounding yourself will help you tune into the practical nature of the Capricorn energy.

Channel your self-discipline & challenge yourself to take responsibility for your actions. Be responsible for creating the change you want to see in the world – stop waiting for someone else to do it!

The Capricorn energy is associated with the 10th house energy of making an impact on the world. What is the legacy you want to leave behind? What are your long-term goals? What do you aspire to be? These questions may come up for you when the moon moves through Capricorn.

Focus on what you'd like to achieve in the long-term. Where would you like to be in 5 years from now? What about 10 or 50 years? Even though it might seem like this is a long time away, it all starts with a seed of intention. Plant that seed today, and imagine where you'll be decades from now!

ꑶ

Capricorn correspondences

Ruling planet: Saturn
Element: Earth
Crystals: malachite, onyx, smoky quartz, hematite, obsidian, jet
Herbs: comfrey, carnation, basil, star anise
Essential oils: pine, tea tree, basil
Body parts: skin, bones, joints
Chakras: root
Tarot: XV The Devil

New moon in Capricorn: Create a strategic plan to achieve your goals. Set intentions for the year ahead. Set intentions for the decade ahead. Focus on your long-term goals.

Waxing moon in Capricorn: Take action towards your long-term goals. Work on a long-term project. Plan how you'll achieve items on your bucket list. Stretch your body with yoga or light exercise.

Full moon in Capricorn: Release the need to control. Celebrate your long-term successes. Relax the entire body with yin yoga, massage or meditation. Show gratitude for what you've manifested over the past 5 or 10 years. Ground yourself with crystals, meditation or connection to nature.

Waning moon in Capricorn: Relax your body. Do yin yoga. Review your long-term goals. Review your strategy, and make adjustments if needed. Focus on grounding practices. Do self-care activities that will help you for the long-term.

Aquarius

+ INNOVATION + COMMUNITY + TEAMWORK +
+ NEW PERSPECTIVES +

Aquarius, ruled by Uranus and air, fuels us to find creative solutions to make the world a better place. With the moon in Aquarius, we may feel like connecting with our communities & friends. This Aquarius energy helps us find new insights & perspectives. We are likely to be more open-minded, ready to try new things.

When the moon is in Aquarius, be open to change & expect the unexpected. Surprises can show up in your life with this Aquarius energy. Be prepared to go with the flow, adjust your plans, and be lead by your intuition.

Be open to new ideas as innovation & creative solutions show us a new way forward in life. Be open to inspiration. New insights & perspectives can come into our lives when the moon transits Aquarius.

Aquarius is associated with the 11th house energy of friendships, community & teamwork. The Aquarius energy helps us understand how we fit into the bigger picture & how we can work together to achieve huge goals. Teamwork makes the dream work!

The Aquarius energy can be selfless, as our focus turns towards the collective rather than the individual. The unique aspects of yourself are often highlighted by the Aquarius energy, but how can you use these unique traits for the benefit of EVERYONE, not just yourself? What gifts can you share with the world to make Earth a better place for all humankind?

♒

Aquarius correspondences

Ruling planet: Uranus
Element: Air
Crystals: garnet, aquamarine
Herbs: ginseng, allspice, cinnamon, clove, coffee
Essential oils: cinnamon, clove
Body parts: ankles
Chakras: root
Tarot: XVII The Star

New moon in Aquarius: Start learning intuitive arts, like astrology or tarot. Set intentions to be more open-minded or inspired. Start a new group or community project. Join a new team.

Waxing moon in Aquarius: Try something new. Take unexpected action. Surprise someone you love. Make changes in your life. Plan how to change the world.

Full moon in Aquarius: Celebrate the things that make you unique. Show gratitude for unexpected abundance. Release chaos. Surprises may manifest into your life. Expect your goals to manifest in unexpected, unconventional or unusual forms.

Waning moon in Aquarius: Let go and follow your intuition. Be open to changes. Don't write a to-do list, just trust your intuition instead. Give back to the community. Perform a random act of kindness. Be open to inspiration. Review new ideas.

Pisces

+ EMOTIONAL SENSITIVITY + DREAMS +
+ INTUITION + SPIRITUALITY +

Pisces, ruled by Neptune and water, is full of emotional & sensitive energy. With the moon in watery Pisces, we feel more in touch with our emotions and subconscious. Our dreams can be vivid, and we can feel more creative. This is a good time for dreaming ahead – dream of your biggest goals.

As dreamy Pisces energy can really fuel your creative fire, the moon in Pisces can be one of the best times in the moon cycle for making music, art, or other creative projects. How can you get into that creative zone? What activities can you do to let your intuition & creativity lead you?

Your intuition is heightened greatly with the moon in Pisces. Pay strong attention to what's coming up in your subconscious – what are you dreaming (or daydreaming) about? What signs is the Universe sending you? You may experience an expanded psychic awareness – like tuning into the thoughts & feelings of those around you, or experiencing clairvoyance.

Pisces is associated with the 12th house energy of spirituality & seeking a deeper meaning to life. What is the deeper meaning behind your goals? Anything that doesn't feel aligned with this deeper meaning will often float away while the moon transits Pisces.

The Pisces energy is an excellent healer, especially on an energetic or emotional level. Listen to your subconscious as you contemplate what energy blocks are stopping you from moving forward. We are more receptive to spiritual healing when the moon moves through Pisces, as we are open to finding more spiritual alignment to our goals.

♓

Pisces correspondences

Ruling planet: Neptune
Element: Water
Crystals: amethyst, larimar, moonstone, aquamarine, ametrine
Herbs: sage, lemon balm, seaweeds, passionflower, lotus, water lily, violet
Essential oils: ylang ylang, lemon balm
Body parts: feet, lymphatic system
Chakras: sacral
Tarot: XVIII The Moon

New moon in Pisces: Pay attention to your subconscious as you plan ahead. Use divination to guide you with your plans for the moon cycle ahead. Make a vision board of your biggest dreams. Meditate to find guidance.

Waxing moon in Pisces: Use tarot cards or astrology to guide you towards taking the most energetically aligned actions. Take inspired action. Meditate & tune into your Higher Self before beginning your work for the day.

Full moon in Pisces: Listen to your dreams, they may be quite vivid. Trust your intuition. Your psychic powers are heightened today. Celebrate your psychic or intuitive powers. Feel grateful for the healing in your life.

Waning moon in Pisces: Heal your energy. Balance your chakras. Play with a creative project. Realign with your dreams & goals for the future. Declutter anything unaligned energetically with what you're manifesting.

ACTIVITY
Discover what sign the moon is in now – there are many apps & websites that quickly tell you, or you can download a free monthly moon calendar from HerbalMoonGoddess.com/Moon-Calendar
Once you know what sign the moon is in, you can pair this knowledge with the moon phase to determine how to direct your energy at this time.
You might like to start a daily journal practice where you record the moon sign & phase, how to work with this energy, and noting down how you feel as well. Notice what comes up for you during different times of the moon cycle as the moon moves through the zodiac.

CHAPTER 6

What The Moon Means For You

Ever wished you could manifest your goals with ease? One part of learning how to manifest external goals is by understanding your internal blueprint. Knowing the moon sign & moon phase you were born under helps you discover this internal blueprint.

It's like laying out all your strengths & weaknesses. It's so much easier when we can focus on our strengths and get help with the stuff we're not so good at!

Maybe you're a Libra moon and you're always indecisive – this indecisiveness can be a weakness, so having an accountability buddy can help you feel more supported in your decisions. Or maybe you're a Pisces moon, and although you can be very creative, you need more stability & structure to help you bring your dreams into reality. Whatever your moon sign is, it will guide you to understand how to manifest with more ease.

In this chapter, you'll discover your personal moon sign & moon phase, and how you can work with that energy to manifest your goals more easily by focusing on the stuff that you're naturally good at & what makes you feel good!

MOON MANIFESTING TIP: When the moon moves into your moon sign, it's like your personal new moon. You can become more deeply aware of your emotions at this time. This can be a good opportunity to work through emotions that are coming up for you – journal, talk with a friend, or quietly reflect & process your emotions. This is an opportunity for emotional renewal. How would you like to FEEL what the lunar cycle ahead?

In my personal observations, I've discovered that when the moon moves into our moon sign, it's like hitting "refresh" on our emotional state. You may notice in the days before the moon moving into your moon sign that you withdraw and reflect on your emotions. Then as the moon moves into your moon sign, you become more aware of these emotions & what's coming up for you subconsciously.

So, what's your moon sign? To find out, you'll need to know the time & date of your birth. If you don't know the exact time, your moon sign may be inaccurate – remember, the moon changes zodiac signs every 2.5 days. If your birthdate happens to be a day when the moon is changing signs, and you don't know the exact time of your birth, you can read through the descriptions of both signs the moon is in on that day to determine which one fits your emotional & inner landscape best.

ACTIVITY
Look up your free astrology chart at astro.com or your favourite astrology website. Then find the moon on your chart (usually symbolized by a crescent moon symbol), and discover which sign the moon is in. You've now discovered your moon sign!

Your Natal Moon Sign

One way to interpret moon signs is that your moon sign describes who you already are, and your sun sign is who you are learning to become. Your moon sign describes who you naturally are, without trying. Your instinctual habits & impulsive reactions often stem from your moon sign.

You'll find some strengths & weaknesses listed for each moon sign. Take what resonates with you and leave what doesn't. Your moon sign is just ONE part of who you are – your complete natal chart can provide much deeper insights into your strengths & weaknesses. However, our moon sign does tell us a lot about ourselves!

You may like to look up the moon sign of your partner, children, parents, or other significant people in your life. This can help you understand their emotional needs better and deepen your relationship with them. I've listed some famous people & their moon signs to help you understand how moon signs can show up in other's personalities, actions, relationships & emotions.

ACTIVITY
Spend time doing activities based on your moon sign. What activities, based on your moon sign, can help you feel emotionally secure? Note how do these activities make you feel. How can you spend more time doing these activities? Find your moon sign on the following pages to discover what activities can help you feel more emotionally secure.

Aries

+ INDEPENDENCE + CREATIVITY + INNER CHILD +
+ IMPULSES +

"The secret of getting ahead is getting started."
- Agatha Christie

STRENGTHS:	WEAKNESSES:
Leadership	Anger, frustration & impatience
Independence	
Creativity	Desires instant gratification or quick results
Taking initiative & acting on impulse	

If your moon is in Aries, you crave instant gratification. Seeing quick results keeps you feeling emotionally satisfied – if tasks start to drag on, or you're not getting the results quick enough, you'll likely get bored and move on. Emotionally, you'll tend to feel that YOUR needs come first. If you don't feel emotionally satisfied, you will be sure to let others know! Aries moon signs can be known for anger outbursts, tantrums, violence, and being temperamental.

Bring more emotional security into your life by finding independence. Relying on others, especially for emotional support, is unlikely to be emotionally nourishing for you. Be your own best friend, and love yourself deeply.

When you are free to follow your impulses is when you feel best. You dislike feeling trapped or restricted – you crave creative freedom. You want to be able to do things in your own unique way.

Creative projects – especially projects that don't take a lot of time or effort – will be especially satisfying for you. Don't be afraid to get your hands messy! There's something childlike about the Aries energy, so channelling your inner child will help you express your Aries moon.

♈

Famous Aries Moons:

- Alecia Beth Moore
- Angelina Jolie
- Bill Gates
- Celine Dion
- Daniel Craig
- Daniel Radcliffe
- Ellen DeGeneres
- Jared Leto
- Joaquin Phoenix
- Pamela Anderson
- Rihanna
- Russell Brand
- Salvador Dali
- Selena Gomez
- Steve Jobs
- Tupac Shakur
- Tyra Banks
- Whitney Houston

Taurus

+ PATIENCE + PRACTICALITY + LUXURIOUS +
+ SENSUALITY +

"Live in each season as it passes; breathe the air, drink the drink, taste the fruit, and resign yourself to the influence of the earth."
- Henry David Thoreau

STRENGTHS:	WEAKNESSES:
Patience	Stubborn
Prefers quality over quantity	Works at a slower pace
Practical & down-to-earth	Resistant to changes
Loyalty & commitment	

If your moon is in Taurus, you feel emotionally secure when you indulge in luxuries. Being frugal or buying "cheap" products probably makes you feel icky or unhappy. Bring more emotional security into your life by focusing on beauty & creating abundance in your life. Regular self-care rituals will help fill your cup – there's probably nothing better than slow soaks in the bath, followed by moisturizing every inch of your skin, then slipping into a soft gown.

Awakening the senses through scents, tastes, textures, sights & sounds will comfort & soothe you. You're likely to bring comforts from home when travelling – like your own toothpaste, food, or pillows!

The Taurus energy is romantic, earthy & practical. Committing to a long-term relationship brings security & safety, especially when there's a strong element of familiarity between yourself & your partner.

Taurus moon signs are patient with emotions. You provide a comforting shoulder to cry on, or a calming friend to talk to. People often describe you as "calm" or "serene" – there's something soothing about your presence.

♉

Famous Taurus Moons:

- Bill Clinton
- Cameron Diaz
- Carl Jung
- Christina Aguilera
- Elle McPherson
- Frida Kahlo
- Jim Morrison
- Joe Biden
- Keira Knightly
- Lindsey Lohan
- Meryl Streep
- Mick Jagger
- Mother Teresa
- Prince Charles, Prince of Wales
- Prince Harry, Duke of Sussex
- Sheryl Crow

Gemini

+ SOCIABLE + CONNECTION + INTELLECTUAL +
+ ADAPTABLE +

"The more you adapt, the more interesting you are."
– Martha Stewart

STRENGTHS:	WEAKNESSES:
Adaptive & flexible	Inconsistency
Open minded	Mood fluctuations
Marketing & networking	Emotional repression
Multi-tasking	

If your moon is in Gemini, you feel emotionally secure when you have a satisfying social life. You may feel easily bored when you have no one to connect with. You love chatting, texting, Snapchatting or otherwise communicating with your network of friends.

You can bring more emotional security into your life by joining social groups of like-minded people (if you're reading this book, you might like to check out some astrology, witchy or manifesting groups on Facebook – or consider joining the Herbal Moon Goddess Academy, my online intuition school).

Regularly connecting with others is also essential for you. Whether that's through online or offline groups, catching up with family, or going out to social events regularly, you'll find emotional satisfaction when you can easily share what's on your mind.

You can be flexible with your emotions which can lead to indecision & changing your mind frequently. Although this adaptability can be a strength, be aware that changing your mind too often can sabotage your efforts. Set your goals & intentions and COMMIT to following through, instead of getting bored along the way and starting something new.

♊

Famous Gemini Moons:

- Barack Obama
- Billy Corgan
- David Schwimmer
- Gwyneth Paltrow
- Hugh Jackman
- Jackie Chan
- Jake Gyllenhaal
- Jennifer Garner
- Jim Carrey
- Kate Beckinsale
- Khloe Kardashian
- Kylie Minogue
- Milla Jovovich
- Rachel McAdams
- Rowan Atkinson
- Sigmund Freud

Cancer

+ MOODINESS + FAMILY + SECURITY +
+ BOUNDARIES + SENSITIVITY +

*"Ah! There is nothing like staying at home
for real comfort."*
- Jane Austen

STRENGTHS:

Sensitivity & intuition

Empathic

Nurturing & caring

WEAKNESSES:

Emotional vulnerability

Holding onto the past

If your moon is in Cancer, you feel emotionally secure when you're nurtured & comfortable. You want to be seen, heard & cared for. Your natural empathy & sensitivity to others emotions helps you comfort & nurture others in your life also.

You feel best when you're at home or with family, so making your home a comfortable sanctuary is essential for you! What would make your home feel more comfortable? Bring more emotional security into your life by creating stable relationships with your family members, and by creating financial security.

Having a regular income that you can depend on is a must-have for Cancer moon signs.

If you don't feel emotionally secure, you may switch to defensive mode. Cancer moons may find it difficult to trust others, especially when it comes to sharing sensitive emotions. However, finding that security allows you to come out of your shell and express your sensitive, sweet self.

As a Cancer moon, you are strongly intuitive, however you may hold yourself back from following your intuition if you feel afraid or insecure about what could happen. You'll often hold yourself back & cling to the past. Don't be afraid to feel what's happening NOW, in the present!

♋

Famous Cancer Moons:

- Adam Sandler
- Catherine, Duchess of Cambridge
- Courtney Love
- Drew Barrymore
- Gwen Stefani
- Heath Ledger
- Isaac Newton
- Jessica Simpson
- Jimi Hendrix
- Keanu Reeves
- Kurt Cobain
- Pierce Brosnan
- Prince William, Duke of Cambridge
- Robert Pattinson
- Shakira
- Taylor Swift

Leo

+ FAME + CREATIVITY + INNER CHILD +

"Only do what your heart tells you."
– Princess Diana

STRENGTHS:	WEAKNESSES:
Creativity	Teamwork
Being in the spotlight	Putting others needs first
Generosity	
Confidence	

If your moon is in Leo, you feel emotionally secure when you are in the limelight. You thrive being in a position of fame or leadership, and you may subconsciously seek to gain popularity. You are confident, and will follow your own path – almost to a point of being stubborn.

Creativity soothes your soul, and you enjoy expressing emotions through the arts – whether that's painting, creating music, or acting. If you're feeling angry, sad or stressed, you could try picking up a paintbrush or musical instrument. It will help to soothe your emotions as you find a creative outlet to express yourself.

The inner child is associated with Leo. As a Leo moon sign, your inner child rules your emotional landscape. Emotionally, you likely get along well with children. Expressing your inner child through fun, play & games is essential for your emotional wellbeing.

♌

Famous Leo Moons:

- Alexander Skarsgard
- Amy Lee
- Bruno Mars
- Charlize Theron
- David Bowie
- Halle Berry
- Helena Bonham Carter
- George Michael
- Julia Roberts
- Kirsten Dunst
- Liam Hemsworth
- Mahatma Gandhi
- Marilyn Manson
- Megan Fox
- Oscar Wilde
- Paris Hilton
- Patrick Swayze
- Paul McCartney
- Queen Elizabeth II
- Tom Cruise
- Tom Hanks
- Winston Churchill

Virgo

+ PERFECTIONIST + ANALYTICAL + CONSISTENT +

"If a man has any greatness in him, it comes to light, not in one flamboyant hour, but in the ledger of his daily work."
- Beryl Markham

STRENGTHS:	WEAKNESSES:
Analysis	Low self-confidence
Being of service to others	Holding yourself back because "it's not perfect"
Editing & reviewing work	Taking criticism deeply
Being consistent, reliable & practical	

If your moon is in Virgo, you may feel overly self-critical, or find yourself analyzing other's emotions. Your emotional landscape demands perfectionism. You may have the self-discipline to practice skills until you master them – however, you may be prone to giving up early if you don't feel that you have natural talent.

Your life must be in order, otherwise you can feel very chaotic & out of control. You might be known as a neat-freak, as you strive to keep your life in strict order. You love to arrive on-time & be punctual. You will often schedule & organize your entire life to a high degree.

You feel best when you make healthy decisions. You know that nourishing your body has an effect on your mental, emotional & spiritual wellbeing. By looking after your own health, you know that it helps you to show up to your full potential so you can be of service to others.

♍

Famous Virgo Moons:

- Courteney Cox
- Chris Hemsworth
- Dolly Parton
- Elon Musk
- Gordon Ramsay
- J. K. Rowling
- Jodie Foster
- John Fitzgerald Kennedy
- John Travolta
- Madonna
- Serena Williams
- Stephen Hawking
- Zac Efron

Libra

+ PEACE + HARMONY + BEAUTY + AESTHETICS +
+ SUPPORT +

"All my life I thought I needed someone else to complete me. Now I know I need to belong to myself."
– Sue Monk Kidd

STRENGTHS:	WEAKNESSES:
Partnership	Dependency on others
Creating peace & calm	Indecision
Pleasing others	Putting other's needs first

If your moon is in Libra, you feel emotionally secure when your life is at peace. You dislike conflict and may strive to always please others. You may play the "peacekeeper" when others are arguing around you. You find more emotional security when you have a partner (whether that's a romantic partner, business partner, or BFF) – you might even notice that you can be clingy at times, as you depend on support & confirmation from a partner. This dependency can make you indecisive with your emotions. You rely on feedback from others to feel secure.

Bring more emotional security into your life by finding independence. Self-love practices will help you feel secure, even if you don't have a partner to support you. Carve out regular space in your schedule for time to fill your cup. Going to a beauty therapist, massage therapist, day spa, or other beauty/wellbeing treatment regularly will help increase your feelings of self-worth & emotional security.

You also find happiness when creating or appreciating arts & music. Bring more emotionally security into your life by creating pleasant aesthetics in your home – focus on your colour schemes, get rid of clutter, and add art or artistic features. Spend more time making art or playing a musical instrument. Bring fresh flowers or scented candles into the home.

If your moon sign is Libra, you'll naturally feel at ease when connecting to others. You know how to charm others, while creating justice & fairness for all.

♎

Famous Libra Moons:

- Alicia Keys
- Anne Hathaway
- Ariana Grande
- Emma Bunton
- George W. Bush

- Harry Styles
- Justin Bieber
- Kate Winslet
- Kristen Stewart
- Leonardo DiCaprio

- Lily Allen
- Mel Gibson
- Nicolas Cage
- Nikola Tesla
- Shania Twain
- Walt Disney
- William Shakespeare

Scorpio

+ MAGNETIC + INTENSE + SENSITIVE +
+ ENERGETIC ALIGNMENT +

"After all, everybody has secrets and there are some things that nobody knows about you but only you, right?"
- Halle Berry

STRENGTHS:

Intuitive sensitivity

Strong inner power

Loyalty

Natural magnetism

Self-transformation

WEAKNESSES:

Secrecy & hidden feelings

Resentment & jealousy

Fears & insecurities

If your moon is in Scorpio, your emotions may feel intense at times. You may be known to be moody, swinging from magnetic happiness to deep broodiness with the drop of a witch's hat. You are naturally sensitive – you can sense other's emotions & energy with ease. You are perceptive and insightful, with the ability to pick up on subtle emotional or energetic clues. You're a natural psychic, telepathic or empathic.

Your emotional intensity can make you very loyal to those you feel close to. You often feel passionate about issues close to your heart. Your need for intimacy can attract people to you – you draw them in with an air of mystery, and magnetize them with your deep sensitivity.

Find emotional security by finding someone who you can express your intimate emotions to. Close relationships that enable you to express your deepest fears & secrets will help you feel more comfortable. Perhaps seeking a counsellor, psychologist or other professional to talk to will lead to further emotional fulfilment & satisfaction, or maybe you prefer regularly expressing your feelings in a journal. Basically, you need a safe space to express the intensity of your emotions. Meditation & introspection will help you move through the depths of your emotions with privacy, as naturally you tend to keep your emotions secretive. Learning to go within, rather than project your emotions on others, can be a valuable tool.

One of your gifts as a natal Scorpio moon is being able to align your energy (or guide others to energetic alignment) to the frequency of your desired outcome. You likely have an understanding of metaphysics and know that energy, thoughts & emotions can manifest in physical form – such as illness, bad luck, poverty or accidents. You find great satisfaction when you are able to help others make energetic shifts to create positive changes in their lives. You may enjoy work as an intuitive reader, healer, counsellor or spiritual coach.

♏

Famous Scorpio Moons:

- Alan Rickman
- Alanis Morissette
- Avril Lavigne
- Beyonce Knowles
- Bjork
- Bob Marley
- Bruce Lee
- Charlie Chaplin
- Elizabeth Taylor
- James Dean
- Jennifer Lopez
- Katy Perry
- Lady Gaga
- Margot Robbie
- Mark Zuckerberg
- Miley Cyrus
- Natalie Imbruglia
- Nelson Mandela
- Orlando Bloom
- Roger Federer
- Ryan Reynolds
- Scarlet Johansson
- Will Smith

Sagittarius

+ OPTIMISTIC + LUCKY + VISIONARY +
+ SPIRITUAL + TEACHER +

"I don't believe in astrology. I'm a Sagittarius, and we're skeptical."
– Arthur C. Clarke

STRENGTHS:	WEAKNESSES:
Adventurous	Commitment
Acts on impulse	False promises
Having faith	Always seeking freedom
Enthusiasm	
Attracting opportunities	

If your moon is in Sagittarius, you feel emotionally secure when you have freedom. There's nothing worse than a Sagittarius moon sign feeling "stuck" – whether it's physically, mentally, emotionally or spiritually. Spend more time travelling, reading books, or studying. You will feel emotionally secure when you're always enrolled or invested in discovering new things, whether that's by attending classes, completing courses, or reading & researching.

Sagittarius moon signs are generally optimistic, happy & lucky. Ruled by Jupiter, you'll naturally uplift others with your cheerfulness. You'll often be inspired with amazing ideas — a natural visionary.

Following a spiritual path will aid you deeply to finding emotional fulfilment. Whether it's through going to church, meditating regularly, or finding your own spiritual path, it's essential for you to have faith in some Higher Being.

As a Sagittarius moon, you love to teach others. You teach from the heart, because you're passionate about your area of expertise. You have possibly devoted years (or decades) of study towards this one area, and love to have deep conversations teaching & discussing it.

Find emotional contentment by spending regular time outdoors & finding new things to experience. Exploring will always fill your heart, so be sure to find freedom through regular road trips, vacations or outings.

♐

Famous Sagittarius Moons:

- Albert Einstein
- Anthony Kiedis
- Charles Dickens
- Charlie Sheen
- Chester Bennington
- Donald Trump
- Emma Watson
- Hilary Duff

- Jennifer Aniston
- Jensen Ackles
- Justin Timberlake
- Lenny Kravitz
- Michael Jordan
- Nicole Kidman
- Oprah Winfrey
- Pablo Picasso
- Richard Gere
- Sharon Stone
- Stephen King
- Ville Valo
- Vin Diesel
- Vincent Van Gogh
- Wolfgang Amadeus Mozart
- Yoko Ono

Capricorn

+ CONTROL + SELF-DISCIPLINE + PRIVACY +
+ CONSERVATIVE +

"I learned the value of hard work by working hard."
- Margaret Mead

STRENGTHS:	WEAKNESSES:
Patience	Controlling
Long-term projects	Judgement on others
Self-discipline	Narrow-mindedness
Strategizing	Negativity

If your moon is in Capricorn, you feel emotionally secure when you feel like you have control over your future. Feeling productive & competent really brings a sense of security for you. You often appear composed, keeping your emotions under control – you are probably known for being able to keep a cool head during stressful times.

In order for you to have this level of emotional composure & control, you require firm boundaries & strong self-discipline. If you notice others taking advantage of you, energetically or physically, you are usually strategic about putting boundaries in place to protect you.

Emotions can be challenging for you, and you probably feel uncomfortable around others who are expressing emotional outbursts. You prefer to just focus on the task at hand, and emotions are an annoying inconvenience at times.

You can bring more emotional security into your life by becoming aware of your emotions. Even if you hide your true feelings from the rest of the world, you are allowed to acknowledge how you really feel. A regular journal practice may help you safely express your emotions in a private space.

♑

Famous Capricorn Moons:

- Abraham Lincoln
- Adolf Hitler
- Amy Winehouse
- Brad Pitt
- Cher
- David Beckham
- Freddie Mercury
- George Clooney
- George Washington
- Johnny Depp
- Jon Bon Jovi
- Kourtney Kardashian
- Matt Damon
- Ozzy Osbourne

- Reese Witherspoon
- Ryan Gosling
- Stevie Nicks
- Tim Burton
- Zooey Deschanel

Aquarius

+ FREEDOM + UNIQUE + SOCIABLE +
+ SURPRISING + UNPREDICTABLE +

"Be yourself; everyone else is already taken."
- Oscar Wilde

STRENGTHS:	WEAKNESSES:
Teamwork	Extremism
Making radical changes	Inner chaos
	Rebellion
Innovative insights	

If your moon is in Aquarius, you feel emotionally secure when you are free to do as you please, unconfined by the restrictions of society. You are likely to be observant of others, analysing why others do what they do, as you feel a sense of detachment from others. It's possible you've always felt "different", especially when you were younger. You may have felt that your emotions are unique, that no-one else could possibly feel what you're feeling.

You might act like you love being social, but really you feel unconnected. You might seem emotionally cold or detached to others at times, however you are great at making friends and probably have a wide network of acquaintances and colleagues. You strive to make sure no-one is left out, fighting for fairness & equality for all. You love to shock & surprise others as you explore unexpected options. Understanding human behaviour is a strength of yours, and you yearn to break the status quo by shaking up the emotional landscape around you. You thrive on unpredictability.

Bring more emotional security into your life by feeling free to be your authentic, quirky self. You know all those weird little traits about you? Share these with the world around you. The chances are that you'll discover there's heaps of other people who love that weird thing about you, or that other people also have this weird unique trait!

♒

Famous Aquarius Moons:

- Ashton Kutcher
- Bill Murray
- Billie Eilish
- Britney Spears
- Eminem
- John Lennon
- Marilyn Monroe
- Morgan Freeman
- Muhammed Ali
- Princess Diana Spencer of Wales
- Russell Crowe
- Tobey Maguire
- Victoria Beckham

Pisces

+ DREAMY + SENSITIVE + EMPATHIC + PSYCHIC +
+ CREATIVE + INTROSPECTIVE +

"Escapism isn't good or bad in itself. What is important is what you are escaping from and where you are escaping to."
- Terry Pratchett

STRENGTHS:	WEAKNESSES:
Creativity & imagination	Separating fiction from reality
Emotional sensitivity	Emotionally driven
Compassion	Confusion
	Guilt
	Anxiety

If your moon sign is in Pisces, you feel emotionally secure when you have time & space to dream. Daydreaming is likely to be a regular habit for you – and it's essential for your creativity & emotional wellbeing! Meditation is also a helpful ally for maintaining your emotional wellbeing. Being creative & artistic will help you express your emotions, so spend more time painting, playing music, doodling, or whatever lights your creative fire.

As a Pisces Moon, you're naturally intuitive. You may be known for your psychic abilities, or discover you have an intuitive gift from an early age.

Bring more emotional security into your life by exploring intuitive arts such as tarot reading, dream interpretation, tea leaf reading, or other forms of divination. Connecting with spirituality will enhance your life – having faith in something bigger than us all brings you a deep sense of security.

You may seem dreamy & introspective but given the right opportunities you can express your dreaminess through creative mediums, like art, music, poetry, or acting. If your creativity is stifled, you may feel emotionally drained or blocked, so you'll likely opt for a career that gives you plenty of creative freedom.

Pisces moon signs are often highly emotionally sensitive. You are likely to be an empath, and have a natural ability for reading others emotions. You have an open heart & an open mind, which can sometimes lead to vulnerability or weakness. It's vital that you create healthy boundaries to ensure others don't take advantage of your compassion & generosity.

The sensitive nature of Pisces moon signs requires that you take plenty of time to retreat to yourself. Introspection is a necessary practice to fulfil your emotion needs.

♓

Famous Pisces Moons:

- Aleister Crowley
- Audrey Hepburn
- Catherine Zeta-Jones
- Coco Chanel
- Elvis Presley
- Frank Sinatra
- Hillary Clinton
- Kanye West
- Kim Kardashian
- Leonardo da Vinci
- Marie Curie
- Martin Luther King
- Michael Jackson
- Michelangelo
- Michelle Obama
- Paul Walker
- Robin Williams
- Sarah Michelle Gellar
- Winona Ryder

Your Natal Moon Phase

The moon phase you were born under describes when your energy & creativity comes to its peak.

You know how some people are great at coming up with ideas, while other people are best at reviewing & adjusting the finer details? Your natal moon phase can help you hone into this natural gift.

Just like discovering your strengths by your moon sign, discovering your moon phase can tell you MORE about your strengths. When we work with our natural strengths, we NATURALLY can manifest easier. Why struggle to do something when it's just not natural for you? Do what you do best and get someone else to help you with the rest. Your natal moon phase helps you understand these natural strengths (and weaknesses) so you can stay within your zone of genius – and manifest your goals faster.

But like anything in astrology, take what resonates with you and leave the rest! Find inspiration in these strengths according to the moon phases, but don't take it too seriously or let it rule your life.

Look up your free astrology chart at astro.com or your favourite astrology website. Find your moon sign. Now find the sun on your chart (usually symbolized by a circle with a dot in the centre). How far away is the moon from the sun? This is how we figure out the moon phase you were born under.

- *If the sun & moon are in the same sign, the moon phase was likely the new moon.*
- *If the moon is within 90 degrees anti-clockwise from the sun, the moon phase was the waxing crescent.*
- *If the moon is approximately 90 degrees anti-clockwise from the sun, the moon phase was the first quarter moon.*
- *If the moon is from 90 to 180 degrees anti-clockwise from the sun, the moon phase was the waxing gibbous.*
- *If the moon is approximately 180 degrees anti-clockwise from the sun, the moon phase was the full moon.*
- *If the moon is from 180 to 270 degrees anti-clockwise from the sun, the moon phase was waning gibbous.*
- *If the moon is approximately 270 degrees anti-clockwise from the sun, the moon phase was last quarter moon.*
- *If the moon is from 270 to 330 degrees anti-clockwise from the sun, the moon phase was waning crescent.*
- *If the moon is from 330 to 360 degrees anti-clockwise from the sun, the moon phase was dark moon.*

New Moon

If your sun & moon are in the same sign, or within 10-20 degrees, your personal moon phase is the new moon.

STRENGTHS:	WEAKNESSES:
Starting new projects	Not following through after the initial enthusiasm wears off
Coming up with new ideas & solutions	
Brainstorming	Daydreaming instead of taking action

Your creativity comes to its peak when you find inspiration in stillness. Meditate, take a nap or just take time off to fuel your creativity. It's this very beginning stage of new projects that you excel at. People come to you for new ideas & solutions. You THRIVE when in the initial stage of projects. Planning, coming up with inspiration, brainstorming, creating a vision board — these ALL spark your creative fires.

Your manifesting power comes from this initial "idea" stage of the manifestation process. Because your power stems from this initial stage of the creation process, you'll find that teaming up with others can help you finalise these ideas so you can manifest your goals. You have that initial "fire" but run out of steam before you can actually bring your ideas into reality. Find an accountability partner, or outsource work to get it finished. Discussing your ideas with a trusted friend can help you refine your ideas & determine which ideas you should follow through with.

Your power hours are during the dawn hours, from around 4am – 8am. Don't be surprised if you wake up feeling inspired by your dreams! These early hours of the morning provide clarity & insight before you start your day. Getting up early for meditation & yoga will fuel your creativity & energy for the day ahead.

Waxing Crescent Moon

If the moon is within 90 degrees anti-clockwise from the sun, the moon phase was the waxing crescent.

STRENGTHS:	WEAKNESSES:
Planning ahead	Stubbornness
Organization skills	Closed off to new ideas
Figuring HOW to manifest your goals	

Your creativity comes to its peak when you have space to daydream & explore new possibilities. You're the one who takes the idea and begins to plan HOW to bring it to life. Planning & organizing feel good for you. You take that initial "spark" of an idea, and begin to plan how to PRACTICALLY bring it into reality.

You're focused on the "how" rather than the "what". Find your inspiration from other sources, then bring that idea to life in your own fashion. You have a strong natural ability to manifest ideas into reality, because you see that idea and just KNOW how to manifest it.

Trust your instincts when it comes to manifesting. The next step can often appear right in front of you, but you might not see it – even when it's literally right under your nose. Inspiration can come from the strangest places. Learning to trust your intuition will help you immensely.

Your power hours are in the early morning from around 7am to 10am. Use this time to journal, plan your day, and feel inspired. Setting goals and intentions in the morning will help you stay inspired. Get yourself a journal and start an inspiring morning ritual!

First Quarter Moon

If the moon is approximately 90 degrees anti-clockwise from the sun, the moon phase was the first quarter moon.

STRENGTHS:	WEAKNESSES:
Taking aligned action	Risk-taking
Going with the flow	Self-sabotage
Taking initiative	Not thinking things through

Your creativity comes to its peak when you take action. You likely find that you can easily "wing it" and just make it up as you go along. It fills your emotional cup to have an active role in projects – you don't like be empty handed or without purpose. You're willing to volunteer and DO things, instead of sitting back waiting for things to happen. You are a natural leader because you make decisions with ease and just get things done.

You can multitask with ease – in fact, you probably find that watching a movie or listening to music while working fuels your creativity. Have a notepad nearby at all times to jot down ideas or sketch your thoughts.

You are often overly confident in your abilities, which can lead to taking risks. Channel your creativity into multiple outlets so you can manifest to a higher potential. When you have excess energy, you may (subconsciously) sabotage yourself. Your moon sign can give you clues about where to channel this excess energy to bring more balance to your life.

Your power hours are around the middle of the day, from around 10am to 2pm. Use this time to make big progress towards your goals. Take aligned action, get in and do the work.

Waxing Gibbous Moon

If the moon is from 90 to 180 degrees anti-clockwise from the sun, the moon phase was the waxing gibbous.

STRENGTHS:	WEAKNESSES:
Hard-working	Leaving tasks to the last minute
Bringing projects to complete	Lack of organization & time-management
Editing & making adjustments	Procrastination

Your creativity comes to its peak when the deadline is looming. You're a "leave it to the last minute" sort of person – because you KNOW that's when you do your best work. You're just not motivated if it's due next month – but if it's due tomorrow, you'll stay up until 3am to get it done. Those late nights fuel your creative fires.

You're willing to go deep into your understanding. You will keep learning, reading & researching so that you feel confident in your knowledge. You strive for perfection and put a lot of effort into your work. You know how to make adjustments to make things more easy or efficient. You strive to make improvements so everything runs better – whether that's improving your skills, your work or your knowledge.

Your power hours are during the early afternoon, from around 1pm to 4pm. You like to push yourself and finish your tasks by the end of the day. Organization will help you meet your goals on time. You may find yourself procrastinating or meeting resistance (which is why you tend to do things at the last minute!). You can harness your natural strengths by jumping in early and getting a head start on your work.

Full Moon

If the moon is approximately 180 degrees (give or take 10-20 degrees each way) anti-clockwise from the sun, the moon phase was the full moon.

STRENGTHS:	WEAKNESSES:
Confidence	Inner conflict & confusion
Connecting with others	Not finding enough time to slow down
Intuitive	
Full of vitality & energy	Lacking clarity

Your creativity comes to its peak when you're in the spotlight. You love to be the life of the party, standing out from the crowd. You're naturally full of vitality. You might be outgoing, extroverted & sociable. You are naturally intuitive and often feel confident just making it up as you go – in fact, this boosts your manifesting efforts, so be sure to follow that intuitive flow when you can!

Your emotional needs can be dynamic, as your moon sign is opposing your sun sign, raising a conflict or division within yourself. This may lead to confusion and not knowing what you want in life.

Although you love to rush in and DO all the things, you can benefit from slowing down, taking a few deep breaths and centring yourself before taking action. A regular meditation practice will assist you greatly with calming your inner chaos & confusion.

Your power hours are in the early evening around sunset – around 4pm through to 8pm. You're the person that has plenty of energy at the end of the day when others around you are exhausted. Channel this excess energy through physical exercise or creative pursuits.

Waning Gibbous Moon

If the moon is from 180 to 270 degrees anti-clockwise from the sun, the moon phase was waning gibbous.

STRENGTHS:	WEAKNESSES:
Collaborating	Overly critical
Sharing with others	Selflessness & giving too much
Providing constructive feedback	Trying to control the outcome
Giving back to the community	

Your creativity comes to its peak when you share with others, editing & making adjustments through this collaborative process. You benefit from sharing your first drafts or prototypes with others for feedback — likewise, you also naturally provide constructive feedback for others as they need it.

Be mindful that you only give feedback when appropriate. You constantly see how the world around you could be improved, but you need to remember that sometimes others aren't ready to change. You have amazing feedback to share, but not everyone is ready to hear it.

You are a natural teacher, as you love sharing your knowledge to help others grow and evolve.

You also naturally strive to help make the world a better place. You love to give back to the community, creating equality & balance for all. You may feel strongly about social issues, or naturally find yourself donating or volunteering to important causes.

Be conscious that you're not giving too much of yourself away. You are naturally compassionate & generous with your time & resources, but you need to remember to reserve some energy for yourself too.

Your power hours are during the evening, from around 6pm through to 10pm. Late nights spent reading & studying satisfy you on a deep level. You also find a lot of satisfaction when you are able to use your time & energy to help others freely – you love being of service to your community.

Last Quarter Moon

If the moon is approximately 270 degrees anti-clockwise from the sun, the moon phase was last quarter moon.

STRENGTHS:	WEAKNESSES:
Reviewing work & editing	Sentimental attachments
Letting go	Living in the past
Decluttering	Feeling stuck

Your creativity comes to its peak when you review & reflect. You are a natural at editing raw material to create a masterpiece. You know how to shed what needs to be released, because you know that by letting go you create space for something even better to manifest. You are a pro at decluttering & cleaning. Organization skills are likely to be a strength for you.

Manifest to a higher potential by knowing when to let go of something. Because you are so great at reflecting on the past, you may find yourself constantly reviewing & remembering past events. While this can be helpful, it can also stagnate your energy. Affirm to yourself that it's safe to let go of the past so you can move forward into a new chapter, cutting out the stuff that's holding you back to make room for something even better to bloom in your life.

Your power hours are during the middle of the night, from around 10pm to 2am. That's because you KNOW the power of a good night's sleep! However, you could be known for midnight snacking (or midnight cleaning – that's a thing, right?) when you feel the calling. You may find that your best ideas come to you when you're trying to fall asleep. Keep a notepad by your bed to jot down this inspiration before sleeping.

Waning Crescent Moon

If the moon is from 270 to 330 degrees anti-clockwise from the sun, the moon phase was waning crescent.

STRENGTHS:	WEAKNESSES:
Introspection	Separating fiction from reality
Intuitive & psychic abilities	Dreaminess
Insights from the subconscious	Feeling alone

Your creativity comes to its peak during self-care & healing practices. It's essential for you to regularly take this time to go inwards and focus on yourself, so you can show up to a higher potential. You'd be amazed at the inspiration you find during a massage, meditation or manicure!

You may have a natural intuitive or psychic ability. You have an immense inner power which you may keep hidden from the world around you – either consciously, or subconsciously because you may not even be aware of your power yet. Trust your intuition & instincts to help you manifest your goals. The Universe will show you the way forward – you just need to ask for the next step.

You are naturally dreamy & imaginative, often lost in a fantasy world – although you can find it difficult to separate this "dream world" from reality. You may often feel alone or isolated, like you don't fit in with the world around you, which can be why you prefer to explore fictional realms.

It's important for you to remember that you are not alone. Perhaps you just haven't found your tribe yet, or maybe you keep your inner self heavily guarded. Try sharing your dreams & imaginative thoughts with others – perhaps through conversations, artworks or creative writing.

Your power hours are during the dark hours of the early morning before the dawn, from around 2am through to 5am. You are possibly a natural for nightshifts, enjoying the stillness and quiet of the darkness. However, deep sleep is important for you, as you may often find deep insights from your dreams at this time.

Dark/Balsamic Moon

If the moon is from 330 to 360 degrees anti-clockwise from the sun, the moon phase was dark moon.

STRENGTHS:	WEAKNESSES:
Healing	Disillusionment
Reflection	Depression & darkness
Tying up loose ends	Detachment

Your creativity comes to its peak during rest. Time away from your regular duties is essential for your creativity – you come back feeling refreshed & renewed, buzzing with new inspiration. Sleep is a priority for you – without proper sleep, you feel drained and uninspired. Avoid caffeine or other stimulants, as these may disrupt your sleep patterns (and thus, disrupt your creative flow!).

Whenever you feel stuck or uninspired, go for a nap or take time off. Vacations can be amazing manifesting opportunities for you – you probably find that you make MORE money whenever you go on vacation.

You are naturally dreamy & intuitive, but you can get lost in your inwards. You may find yourself trapped under a (metaphorical) cloud of darkness at times. When your reality doesn't live up to your expectations, you can easily feel disconnected & depressed.

You generally stay disconnected from current events in the world – you prefer to hibernate in your safe little bubble. This detachment helps you keep your emotions under control. All the fighting, crime & fear in the world affects you deeply, so you find it easier to just stay away from it.

You have a natural instinct for bringing things to an ending or completion. You thrive on tying up loose ends. You know that endings bring new beginnings. When one door closes, another opens. You may relate to the phoenix, rising from the ashes. Rebirth & transformation are powerful tools for you.

Shadow work can be a powerful ally to help you transform your inner darkness and help you heal. Explore your inner realms and bring your darkness to light. You find strength in being about to transform negative energy into positive vibrations.

Your power hours are just before daybreak – the hours may vary depending on the season, but generally 4am to 6am. Rising before daybreak for meditation, yoga or quiet contemplation will help you start your day feeling in tune with the Universe.

CHAPTER 7

Eclipses

+ TRANSFORMATION + SOUL GROWTH +
+ LIFE LESSONS +

If you've ever observed an eclipse, you'll know first-hand the intense energy they bring. Eclipses are not only a spectacular sight to see, but also an intense thing to feel. In the past (you know, before science and stuff) people were scared of and actually FEARED eclipses. They were thought to be times of very bad luck, a bad omen.

However, I view eclipses as portals of transformation. When you discover how to use this eclipse energy, you can consciously use the power of eclipses to create dramatic (but positive) changes in your life.

Eclipses occur during a ~35 day window every ~6 months, when the moon crosses the path of the sun (also known as the ecliptic). Eclipses can occur 4-6 times per year – so while they may be seen as rare events, they DO happen with regularity multiple times per year.

That being said, you may not be able to see all of the eclipses from your usual place of residence, as the path of the eclipse will vary.

Eclipses will often come in pairs or triplets, as any new or full moon that falls in that 35 day period will align with the sun. It's not unusual to experience a lunar eclipse with a solar eclipse following two weeks a later (or vice versa – the solar eclipse could happen first, then a lunar eclipse!). As the lunar cycle takes about 29 days, it's absolutely possible to experience 3 eclipses in this 35 day window if the timing lines up.

Solar Eclipses

Solar eclipses occur when the moon moves directly in the path of the sun, blocking out the light for a short time. Solar eclipses are powerful manifesting portals. These are strong opportunities for manifesting great changes in your life, propelling you towards your greater destiny.

Solar eclipses occur in conjunction with a new moon. The path of the eclipse (ie. where the solar eclipse is visible from) is quite specific, often being contained to one small part of the world. It's not unusual for the path of solar eclipses to fall around either the North or South Poles, or somewhere around the equator, depending on the time of year. To actually see a total solar eclipse with your own eyes is a rare event! However, partial or annular solar eclipses are often visible from more populated areas of the world. Still, to see a solar eclipse is often a matter of being in the right place at the right time.

However, whether you can see a solar eclipse or not, you can still tune into the intense energy of this event. You don't need to travel to Antarctica to catch the next total solar eclipse to harness the energy of this powerful manifesting portal!

Solar eclipse journal prompts:
- What new opportunities am I ready to manifest into my life?
- What new life am I dreaming of?
- What changes am I ready to commit to?

Questions to ask your cards on the solar eclipse:
- What am I ready to manifest into my life?
- What obstacles am I ready to dissolve?
- What action do I need to commit to so I can manifest my goal?

Action steps for the solar eclipse:
- **Set your intentions.** This is a potent time for intention setting. Find clarity through meditation so you can set clear & strong intentions for this eclipse energy. Focus on the changes you wish to create over the next 6 months.

- **Be ready to create change**. Solar eclipses can trigger powerful changes to occur QUICKLY. Don't underestimate this power. Be careful what you wish for on a solar eclipse! This energy will require you to make deep transformation & to step out of your comfort zone.

Lunar eclipses

Lunar eclipses occur when the Earth blocks the light of the sun onto the moon, casting a shadow. As you may have guessed, lunar eclipses occur during a full moon. Lunar eclipses create powerful portals of release. This is a great time for releasing yourself from the past, cutting cords, and removing anything that's unaligned with your soul's true path.

Unlike viewing solar eclipses, where you need to be in the right place at the right time, lunar eclipses are somewhat easier to view. If it's night time in your area when the lunar eclipse is occurring, chances are that you'll be able to view it. Lunar eclipses are often visible in most parts of the world (although sometimes an entire continent can miss out if the timing isn't right!). Total lunar eclipses transform the moon into a beautiful blood-red shade, however partial or penumbral eclipses will have a more subtle visual effect.

However, just like solar eclipses, you don't need to view the lunar eclipse to harness the energy of this portal of transformation.

Lunar eclipse journal prompts:
- What's holding me back from my higher potential?
- What do I want to transform & release from my life?
- What will my life feel like after this release?

Questions to ask your cards on the lunar eclipse:
- What's the next chapter for my soul's path?
- What feelings am I ready to transform?

- What is no longer aligned with my desired life?

Action steps for the lunar eclipse:
- **Perform a releasing ritual.** This is a powerful time for releasing what's no longer aligned with who you want to become. What's holding you back from your higher potential? You'll find directions for a releasing ritual in the Full Moon chapter.

- **Move your body.** Release your emotions & thoughts with a long yoga session, or try dancing it off. Our emotions get stored in our physical body, so to release them we need to move our body! Move however you feel called to. You'll notice a shift in your energy as you release it all out.

So, how do you harness the energy of eclipses?

First up, you'll want to identify what it is that you wish to transform in your life. In the lead up to an eclipse, we'll often naturally see what needs to be changed. Eclipses can stir up chaos in our lives, so sometimes it's really clear what needs to be transformed. Solar eclipses bring transformation through manifestation, and lunar eclipses bring transformation through releasing.

At other times, meditation, tarot reading or journaling can be useful practices to help us tune into our inner self so we can find what we are ready to transform. Reading your horoscope can also give you insights (Hint: check which house the eclipse is falling in on your natal chart! This will tell you the area of your life that is in focus for this eclipse).

Be careful what you wish for though! Sometimes these changes can happen a lot quicker than we expect. Eclipses trigger growth, transformation, and stepping out of your comfort zone. Both lunar & solar eclipses push us towards our future destiny, encouraging us to leave the past behind.

Once you know EXACTLY what you want to transform in your life, send that intention out to the Universe. You can do this through meditation, repeating affirmations, chanting, writing it out, or with a symbolic ritual. Or, just simply say out loud, "Universe, this is what I want to manifest/release!". Declare it loud and proud, find confidence in the transformation you are beginning.

Visualize how it would feel once that transformation has happened in your life. Feel it in every cell of your body. Bring the vibration of what you want to manifest into your body.

If you want to manifest a new home, imagine how it would feel to be in your new space! Visualize the rooms, the furniture, the smells, the sounds. Visualize yourself walking through your new home. Let yourself be immersed in the details – what does this new home feel like for you?

If you want to manifest money, feel into how being wealthy makes you feel. What would you have the financial freedom to do? What would more money change about your life? Perhaps you'll feel the relief of no more debts. Perhaps you'll feel more comfortable as you'll have the financial means to buy more luxurious items.

Whatever you want to manifest with the eclipse, bring that feeling into your body, as though it had already manifested.

To finish your eclipse ritual, get physical. When you move your body, it helps bring that vibration from your mental state into your physical. That's exactly what we're doing when we're manifesting – we're transforming thoughts into physical matter! So get moving with a yoga flow, dancing, going for a walk, or whatever feels good for you.

But really, there's no right or wrong way to do an eclipse ritual. Do whatever feels good to YOU. Simply thinking about your intentions can be enough to create a shift.

As a demonstration of just how powerful eclipses are, let me share with you a story of how I manifested $50,000.

At the time, money was really tight for us. We were in debt, and our income was barely enough to live on. On a lunar eclipse, I stood under the blood red moon and prayed to the Universe that our financial debts would no longer be a burden.

The morning after, I woke up and checked my bank account, worrying that bills have been debited & that I'd have no money to buy our weekly groceries. To my dismay, a $800 bill had been direct debited from our account – and we were in the negative. We literally had NO money, and our credit cards were maxed out.

I moped around for a while and tried to sell some stuff online to bring us more money. I was trying to stay positive. I tried shifting my energy with some yoga - I remember standing in tadasana, gazing up at Father Sky silently repeating "Thank you Father Sky, thank you Father Sky, thank you Father Sky!". Just trying to stay positive, even though I was so worried about our lack of money.

Then my husband got a phone call to confirm an amount of $50,000 would be paid into our account within the WEEK!

What a shift from literally having no money to feed our family, to receiving a significant lump sum. Some might say it was a coincidence, but I don't believe in coincidences. The timing was too Divine. I truly believe that the energy of the eclipse, plus my intentions & prayers, helped this money manifest into my reality.

Although eclipses can be so POWERFUL for manifesting changes into your life, the energy can feel quite overwhelming & unstable, especially in those weeks between eclipses in an eclipse season (remember, eclipses always come in pairs or triplets!).
It's so important to stay grounded during eclipse season to help you integrate these deep changes that are occurring for you. Do yoga, carry grounding crystals like black tourmaline, tiger's eye, hematite & smoky quartz, and spend quiet time in nature. Solitude can help you integrate this eclipse energy.

CHAPTER 8

When The Moon Is Void Of Course

+ PRODUCTIVITY + MAINTENANCE +

There's something else which is super important to understand about working with the moon, and that's tracking when the moon is void of course.

In astrology, we're looking at the angles that the planets are making with each other. You may have heard about Jupiter conjoining Saturn, or the Sun making a challenging square with Mars, or other similar events. The angles spark the energy to flow between planets, triggering events to happen here on Earth.

The moon also makes angles, sparking emotional activity to happen in our lives (remember, the moon rules our emotions!). But when there's no angles to fire off this lunar energy, well...things start to get a bit dull. From the time the moon makes its last angle to a planet before moving into the next zodiac sign is what we call the moon being void of course. There's no more angles for the moon to make while it's in that current zodiac sign.

So let's say the moon is currently in Scorpio. As the moon moves through Scorpio, it might oppose Uranus, then make a trine with Mars, but then it won't make any angles with any other planets until it moves into Sagittarius. So from the time the moon in Scorpio makes the trine with Mars until the moon moves into Sagittarius is known as a void-of-course moon.

I know this can seem complex and confusing, so don't worry if you don't understand how it works right off the bat! But trust me! Knowing when the moon is void-of-course will help you a lot.

I personally never used to take much notice of the times that the moon was void of course, but I've followed it pretty religiously for the past year or so now, and I've noticed what a difference this makes. Knowing what & what NOT to do when the moon is void of course can help you boost your productivity levels while providing time for self-care & rest. For me, it's brought more balance into my life.

So how do you know if the moon is void of course? There are some apps that can tell you, or you may like to find a moon/astrology diary which lists the times of the void-of-course moon. I release an annual Moon Manifesting Planner which lists when the moon is void-of-course (along with other daily moon & astrology related information), which has become a daily tool for hundreds of moon lovers to align their life with the magick of the moon.

Now that you know how to determine if the moon is void-of-course, the next thing you should know is what you should & shouldn't be doing during this time.

156

When the moon is void-of-course, it's a good time for catching up on housework, doing yoga, meditating, or just "taking time off" – maybe go for a stroll in nature, or chillout with Netflix. Find that balance in your life! If you do need to focus on business stuff, spend time working on admin tasks or other behind-the-scenes work.

Avoid scheduling important appointments or events when the moon is void-of-course – often things won't go to plan, and it will be a waste of time. I block off my calendar when the moon is void-of-course, because I know that clients might not show up, or my intuition could be off and the reading could just come out all wrong. I won't risk it.

Focus on doing the stuff that needs doing over and over again anyway. I view this time as excellent for maintenance – whether that's doing the dishes, fixing the backend of your website, doing admin work like data entry, or spiritual maintenance like meditation.

I love planning my life according to when the moon is void-of-course, because it allows me to take regular time away from work tasks or structured routines. When the moon is void-of-course in the mornings, I love sleeping in late - totally guilt-free. If there's a few hours during the day when the moon is void-of-course, I'll go play with the kids or get creative.

The thing is, you can't really plan what to do during the void-of-course moon. Because your plans probably won't work out how you intended! When there's a significant void-of-course moon period coming up, like 9 hours during the day, I'll often create a mental list of things that I COULD do. But I drop my expectations that any of those things will happen. Just go with the flow when the moon is void-of-course. Sometimes stuff happens that you can't control – don't stress about it!

Basically, when the moon is void of course and there's something I need to do, I ask myself:
- Do I want to do this task again? Is it something that I'll need to do again anyway? If yes, it's probably safe to do this when the moon is void-of-course.
- Is this an important task or appointment? Do I only get one shot at this and want it to work out successfully? If yes, it's probably better to wait until the moon is not void-of-course.

It's fun to note that if there is an important appointment or something similar which you DO want to avoid, schedule it for when the moon is void-of-course. You'll likely discover that the other person cancels, you get sick, or something else happens and the appointment gets delayed. I knew someone who had to go to court, and I discovered their court hearing was scheduled for when the moon was void-of-course. I told them that the hearing would probably get adjourned to a later date. And that's exactly what happened!

You can absolutely work this knowledge to your advantage by turning these void-of-course windows into play time. Do you want to have more fun & spend more time playing? Of course you do! And if you answered no to that question, that's a strong sign that you actually NEED to spend more time playing, having fun, getting creative, or just having time to relax.

By asking yourself, "What do I want to do more of?", you can get a good idea of the activities you could enjoy when the moon is void-of-course. Personally, I love spending that moon void-of-course time to focus on self-care activities. Have a long bath, journal, pull some tarot cards, meditate, read an enlightening book, spend time in the garden, play with the pets or children.

However, don't try to plan these things in advance! As previously mentioned, things often don't go to plan when the moon is void-of-course. It's best if you just keep your schedule free, and you can follow your intuition when the time comes. Maybe you'll feel drawn to catching up with a friend, heading outdoors somewhere, playing with paints or music, or maybe you'll just feel like having a nap. Do what FEELS good in the moment. Go with the flow.

As the moon can be void-of-course quite irregularly, occurring every 2-3 days, from 15 minutes up to 2 days, sometimes it catches you by surprise. There's been mornings when I start tackling my to-do list and nothing goes to plan, then suddenly I realise that the moon is void-of-course. So I switch my focus, decide to come back to these tasks later, and go with the flow. Why struggle with something that's just not going with the flow?

Knowing when the moon is going to be void-of-course is a great productivity hack. If you want to be more productive and spend your time more efficiently, knowing when the moon is void-of-course (and acting accordingly!) will help you significantly.

CHAPTER 9

The Moon & Your Everyday Life

+ RITUALS + ASTROLOGICAL HOUSES +

So now we can take this knowledge of working with the moon, and venture a layer deeper.

If you've ever looked at your natal chart, you may have noticed the astrological houses. Astrology is basically just layers upon layers – the planets are the energy being expressed, the zodiac signs are how the energy is expressed, and the astrological houses explain which area of your life the energy is being expressed.

Planet = **WHAT** energy is being expressed
Zodiac = **HOW** the energy is expressed
House = **WHERE** in your life the energy is expressed

This whole book is about the moon, so we're talking about the moon's energy of emotions, instincts & security. We've just covered HOW these emotions & instincts are being expressed throughout the month by checking in with the zodiac signs.

The next step is to determine which part of your life is being affected, the WHERE of this equation. This is what the astrological houses tell us.

So a full moon in Scorpio could suggest releasing – because full moons can be about release & letting go. The Scorpio energy suggests a releasing of fears & insecurities, but for one person it could be fears about money, and for another person it might be fears about their health, and yet another person could be feeling these fears in their relationships – and this all comes down to the houses.

By looking at which house the moon is falling in for you each day, you can get an idea of which area of your life is under the spotlight. This will help you understand when the best times are for manifesting specific things, or where your energy will be naturally directed. Isn't life so much easier when we work WITH the natural cycle of the moon?

There are many different house systems in astrology. Chances are if you've had an astrology chart done for you (or you've looked up your own chart), it will be based on the Placidus house system, which has been used for hundreds of years. This is the most commonly used house system in Western astrology. The Placidus house system begins your 1st house from the ascendant, or rising sign, based on the time you were born.

You can also look at your sun houses & moon houses as you're checking in with the moon each day.

Find your sun sign, then count anti-clockwise around the chart. So if you're a Gemini sun, Gemini is your 1st sun house, Cancer is your 2nd sun house, Leo is your 3rd house, and so forth – keep counting until you get to the 12th house. Do the same for your moon sign by starting in the zodiac sign that your moon is in, and count around the chart.

Your rising sign house signifies which area of your life is being activated. Your sun house signifies which area of your life is coming into your consciousness or focus. Your moon house signifies which area of your life is coming into your subconscious or emotional focus.

For example, my rising sign is Scorpio, my sun sign is Gemini and my moon sign is Libra.

When the moon is in:	My rising sign house is:
Scorpio	1st
Sagittarius	2nd
Capricorn	3rd
Aquarius	4th
Pisces	5th
Aries	6th
Taurus	7th
Gemini	8th
Cancer	9th
Leo	10th
Virgo	11th
Libra	12th

When the moon is in:	My sun house is:
Gemini	1st
Cancer	2nd
Leo	3rd
Virgo	4th
Libra	5th
Scorpio	6th
Sagittarius	7th
Capricorn	8th
Aquarius	9th
Pisces	10th
Aries	11th
Taurus	12th

When the moon is in:	My moon house is:
Libra	1st
Scorpio	2nd
Sagittarius	3rd
Capricorn	4th
Aquarius	5th
Pisces	6th
Aries	7th
Taurus	8th
Gemini	9th
Cancer	10th
Leo	11th
Virgo	12th

Note: I've simplified these tables by using whole sign houses. Usually you'll find each zodiac sign moves through 1-2 houses.

So if the moon is in Pisces, the moon is in 5th rising sign house, my 10th sun house & my 6th moon house. This highlights my external focus, my conscious focus & my subconscious focus while the moon moves through Pisces. So I know that when the moon is in Pisces, externally I'll be focusing on fun, creativity & play (the 5th house energy). Consciously I'll be focusing on my career or impact (the 10th house energy). Subconsciously, I'll be focusing on my health or daily routines (6th house energy).

ACTIVITY

Create your own table/chart so you can easily see which houses fall in each zodiac sign, based on your own rising sign, sun sign & moon sign.

A daily ritual you could try is checking which sign the moon is in, and which sun house, rising sign house & moon house the moon is in. The rising sign house signifies what area you'll naturally be gravitating to. The sun house signifies what area you'll consciously be focused on. The moon house signifies what area your creativity & emotions will be focused on. Try recording these in a journal, and note how you're feeling, what you're working on, or anything else significant.

1ˢᵗ House

+ IDENTITY + APPEARANCE + AUTHENTICITY +

The 1ˢᵗ house is about discovering our identity. We can feel very self-aware when the moon is moving through our 1ˢᵗ house. We focus on who we are, who we want to be, and how we appear to others.

Associated with Aries and ruled by Mars, the 1ˢᵗ house can make you feel in tune with your inner self. You feel more comfortable to express yourself authentically, having courage to share your individual views. You'll feel a surge of motivation, determination & drive when the moon moves through your 1ˢᵗ house. There's a strong energy of new beginnings, with a wave of enthusiasm to push you forward on this new cycle.

The moon transiting your 1ˢᵗ house brings your attention to who you are & who you want to be. How are you asserting yourself? How do others portray you? You may find yourself focusing on your personal appearance – your clothes, your hair, or your makeup. You may also naturally be drawn to self-discovery, perhaps through journaling, reading your natal chart, doing personality quizzes, or contemplating the question, "Who am I?".

When the moon is in your 1ˢᵗ house, choose to focus on yourself. Put your own needs first. Be confident to express your own opinion and to go after your own desires. Have the ambition to push forward in the direction that YOU want to go.

When the moon is in your 1st house, ask yourself:

- Who are you? Who do you identify as?
- Who do you want to be?
- How do you portray yourself to the world? How do others see you?
- How do you want to be portrayed & seen by others?

2ⁿᵈ House

+ GOALS + DESIRES + VALUES +

The 2ⁿᵈ house is about what we desire & value. Our goals come into our focus as we discover what we truly want to manifest.

Associated with Taurus and ruled by Venus, the 2ⁿᵈ house explores the physical & practical things in life that we desire. When the moon moves through the 2ⁿᵈ house, the sensual pleasures in life are brought to our focus. Money, beauty, possessions & relationships are all associated with this 2ⁿᵈ house energy.

When the moon transits the 2ⁿᵈ house, we desire more pleasure & luxury in our lives. What do you really want in your life? What physical or tangible things would you like to manifest?

When the moon is moving through your 2ⁿᵈ house, get clear on your goals, values & desires. Indulging in luxuries with help you feel more abundant & prosperous, and when you vibrate at that level you can attract MORE abundance & luxury into your life. Manifesting your goals is your biggest focus with the moon in your 2ⁿᵈ house.

When the moon is in your 2ⁿᵈ house, ask yourself:
- What are your goals?
- What do you highly value in your life?
- If money was no issue, what would you have in your life?
- How do you manifest your goals?

3rd House

+ COMMUNICATION + NETWORKING +

The 3rd house is about our connections, networks, and how we express our ideas. Associated with Gemini, this house is about connecting to people who can help us reach our goals faster. Collaborate, ask for help, share your thoughts, work in a team. Combine strengths to make an even stronger partnership.

Ruled by Mercury, the 3rd house focuses on communication & sharing your message with others. Naturally, we feel more communicative when the moon is moving through our 3rd house. We'll feel more comfortable expressing our emotions & feelings with others.

You'll naturally feel like talking about your ideas & opinions when the moon is moving through your 3rd house. Use this energy towards marketing, networking on social media or in person, writing blog posts, recording podcasts, sending newsletters, or other communication tasks.

Plan your social events for when the moon is moving through your 3rd house, as you'll naturally feel like connecting & networking with others during this time.

When the moon is in your 3ʳᵈ house, ask yourself:

- Who can help you?
- What are your weaknesses? Who has strengths to match your weaknesses?
- What do you need to communicate to help you reach your goal?

4th House

+ HOME + FAMILY + SECURITY +

The 4th house is about our home & family life, and about creating security with our emotions & money. Bring comfort into your life so you can feel more nurtured & cared for.

Associated with Cancer, the 4th house can turn our focus inwards as we contemplate our emotions. Insecurities and negativity may arise, but this is a good time for bringing in positive vibes so you can feel more confident & comfortable with your life. Self-love practices during this time will help boost your positivity.

Ruled by the Moon, the 4th house brings up emotions, mother or parenting issues, our home & family life, and how we react to situations. We may find ourselves needing extra nurturing when the moon moves through our 4th house. This can be a time of the month when we turn towards eating comfort foods, or we may be feeling a bit moody.

Focus on bringing comfort into your life when the moon is transiting your 4th house. What would make you feel secure – on a physical or emotional level?

When the moon is in your 4th house, ask yourself:
- What would make you feel more comfortable & secure?
- What negative thoughts have been coming up lately?
- How can you love & nurture yourself more?

5ᵗʰ House

+ CREATIVITY + FUN + INNER CHILD +

The 5ᵗʰ house is about fun, play & creativity. Discover your inner child & connect with what your inner child desires. How can you spend more time having fun?

Associated with Leo and ruled by the Sun, the 5ᵗʰ house helps us shine our light into the world. How can you inspire others? Where can you find more motivation? The 5ᵗʰ house highlights how you can shine to your fuller potential.

Explore your creative side. What are you feeling called to create? Design, paint, bake or make – it's up to you. Have fun as you follow your creative passions.

When the moon is transiting your 5ᵗʰ house, have more fun in your life. Make a bit of time for play or to pursue your creative hobbies. Channel your inner child, laugh and find joy in life!

When the moon is in your 5ᵗʰ house, ask yourself:
- How can you have more fun today?
- What creative project would you like to work on?
- What is your inner child calling you to do?

6th House

+ HEALTH + WORK + ROUTINES +

The 6th house is about routines, health & day-to-day physical activities.

Associated with Virgo and ruled by Mercury, the 6th house helps you look after yourself so you can serve others to your highest potential. Is your cup feeling empty, or are you serving from your overflow? Focus on nourishing yourself so you can feel better.

Your health issues can come to the surface when the moon transits your 6th house. This can be an ideal time to work on healing pre-existing health conditions, or making healthy choices. Eat well, move your body, meditate, and get adequate sleep. You may notice habits that are affecting your health. When the moon moves through your 6th house, you can change up these habits and start swapping unhealthy choices for healthier ones.

Your daily routines may also come to your conscious attention when the moon is in your 6th house. You'll notice how you go about your day, and how you can improve the efficiency of your life. Maybe you'll discover a better route to travel to your destination, or perhaps you'll feel call to change your bedtime or waking time to better suit your needs.

When the moon is transiting your 6th house, healing may come into your focus. Notice what's coming up for healing during these days. Perhaps there's physical symptoms that require your attention, or maybe it's emotional healing that you require. Appointments with health care providers or healers during this time can be extremely beneficial. You'll be more likely to commit to your health with the moon in your 6th house.

When the moon is in your 6th house, ask yourself:

- How can you nourish your body, mind & soul?
- What do you feel like healing today?
- What routines are serving you? What routines would you like to change?

7ᵗʰ House

+ RELATIONSHIPS + SUPPORT +

The 7th house is about relationships, and how we give & receive support. Although relationships are the focus on the 7th house, it's important to remember that a partnership is only as strong as the partners. Focus on your strengths, and how you can combine strengths with someone else to create a strong partnership. What strengths do YOU bring to your partnerships?

Associated with Libra and ruled by Venus, the 7th house reminds us to take time out for self-care practices. We can't show up and support others to our full potential if our cup is half-empty. We need to love and support OURSELVES just as much as we love and support others in our lives.

The moon transiting your 7th house brings relationships to your emotional focus. The days that the moon is in your 7th house are great opportunities for romance, going on a date, or building stronger relationships.

When the moon is in your 7th house, consider how you can support others in your life. Who are the people closest to you – your partner, children, parents, siblings, best friends? What support do these people need from you today? Or how would you like to support these people?

Similarly, consider how YOU need more support in your life. What do you need in your life so you feel more supported & loved? What support would help you move to the next level? Support could be in the form of help around the house, virtual assistance for your business, or finding a mentor or coach.

When the moon is in your 7th house, ask yourself:
- What support do you need and who can give you that support?
- Who needs your support today?
- How can you bring more love (including self-love) into your life?

8th House

+ BUSINESS + FINANCES + SHADOW WORK +
+ MYSTERIES +

The 8th house is about the mysteries & hidden parts of our lives. This is the part of our life that we repress or maybe feel "isn't good enough" to share with the rest of the world. There's an introspective energy to the 8th house that calls us to withdraw, go within & explore our secret fears.

Associated with Scorpio and ruled by Mars & Pluto, the 8th house covers a range of areas including business, finances, shadow work, repressed feelings, sex & intimacy, and death. You could view this as exploring the unfamiliar parts of ourselves to transform our innermost insecurities into a source of power & strength. The 8th house energy helps us evolve, transform & rebirth ourselves.

The moon in the 8th house brings awareness to what we want to change in our lives. What emotions have been holding you back? Transform your self-doubt into confidence. Find your inner power.

We can feel our emotions more intensely when the moon is transiting our 8th house. As our emotions come to the surface, we can more easily process and transform these inner feelings. This transit is an ideal time for doing shadow work, as you will be naturally able to access your deeper inner workings. Transform your emotions from darkness and negativity into love and light.

As the 8th house is also associated with the energy of business and making other people's money YOUR money, this can be a good time for focusing on income-producing activities. What's the easiest way for you to make money? What can you improve in your business or money-making activities?

When the moon is in your 8th house, ask yourself:
- What fears, insecurities or repressed emotions are coming up for transformation?
- How could you feel more secure in your life?
- How would you like to evolve?

9th House

+ EDUCATION + EXPLORATION +

The 9th house is about exploring on a deeper level. This is where we go DEEP into topics of interest. We read or watch tutorials. We learn new skills. We gain a deeper understanding to life.

Associated with Sagittarius and ruled by Jupiter, the 9th house prompts you to explore – through travel, education, or spirituality. Find freedom through empowering yourself with knowledge. There is a craving to KNOW MORE when the moon moves through the 9th house. How can you deepen your wisdom & understanding?

We feel positive and optimistic when the moon transits our 9th house. We often have faith that everything will work out perfectly. We connect more deeply to our spiritual practices.

When the moon transits the 9th house, our curiosity is sparked. Follow your passions, learn as much as you can, and share your knowledge with others. Teaching comes naturally, or you may find yourself deep in a philosophical discussion with others. This is a time of learning and teaching, expanding your horizons.

Some activities that are suited for when the moon is transiting the 9th house include meditation, yoga, reading, learning, working at your altar (or setting up an altar), traveling, or connecting to a deity. Find deep purpose in what you do.

When the moon is in your 9th house, ask yourself:
- What do I want to learn more about?
- Where do I want to travel to?
- How can I reconnect with my spiritual practices?

10ᵗʰ House

+ CAREER + LEGACY + IMPACT +

The 10th house is about our legacy and the impact we strive to make in the world. These are our aspirations, how we naturally strive to feel each day as we take steps towards

Associated with Capricorn and ruled by Saturn, the 10th house brings your focus to your career & long-term aspirations. How can you challenge yourself & be self-disciplined to work hard towards your long-term goals?

The moon moving through your 10th house helps you feel motivated to work hard towards your goals, knowing that your hard work will pay off. Challenge yourself when the moon is in your 10th house. Have the self-discipline to follow through with consistency.

The 10th house energy captures the essence of what we strive to be in our lives. You'll work hard to achieve your personal goals – even if these goals are subconscious.

When you look to the future, how do you envision yourself? What does the future you look like? You'll naturally be working towards manifesting this vision when the moon moves through your 10th house.

When the moon is in your 10th house, ask yourself:
- What are your long-term goals?
- What do you aspire to be, do or have?
- How are you feeling about your career?

11th House

+ COMMUNITY + TEAMWORK + FRIENDSHIPS +

The 11th house is about community & friendships. This house describes how we connect with others — within our wider circles, or within group settings.

Associated with Aquarius, the energy of the 11th house is about making the world a better place for all. It's about daring to be different, following innovative sparks, and thinking outside the box. Ruled by Uranus, the 11th house sparks those quirky, unusual aspects of ourselves.

The moon in the 11th house helps us find security in being unique, seeing how we fit into the bigger picture. We want to connect with like-minded souls who share our vision. When the moon is in your 11th house, go out and connect with others. Participate in online discussions. Meet up with friends. The 11th house can make us feel more sociable and friendly. How do you fit into society? Where's your place in the bigger picture?

Our hopes & wishes for ALL humankind can come to our focus when the moon transits the 11th house. How can we change the world so it's a better place for everyone? We feel like co-operating to meet mutual goals and to bring equality & fairness to the world around us.

When the moon moves through your 11th house, zoom out and see the bigger picture. Life is not just about YOU. We're all in this together — but we each have our own roles to play. What's your role within your community?

When the moon is in your 11th house, ask yourself:

- How can you connect with your friends, groups or community today?
- How do you fit into the bigger picture? What's your place in society?
- How can you make the world a better place today?

12th House

+ DEEPER PURPOSE + SPIRITUALITY + REST +

The 12th house is about the deeper purpose in life. As the final house in the zodiac wheel, the 12th house signifies an ending. After moving through the other 11 houses, exploring different areas of our lives, it's now time to integrate what we've learnt this cycle.

Associated with Pisces and ruled by Neptune, the 12th house asks us to explore spirituality. We are called to find the purpose & meaning behind what we are manifesting in our lives.

With the moon in your 12th house, you may feel like withdrawing from the world and becoming more introspective. Your emotions may be overwhelming, and you may just need some alone time. This is the perfect time in the moon cycle for you to take some time off. Relax, recharge & reset before your energy cycle renews again when the moon moves into your 1st house.

Confusion may occur when the moon is transiting your 12th house. Illusions and deceptions may blur your focus, and you may feel like you've lost your way. You may even find yourself questioning, "Who am I?" and "What am I doing with my life?". Remember that this is a time of renewal, so allow yourself to process these deep questions. It might be helpful to journal, consult your tarot cards, or meditate.

Tune out from the world around you so you can tune into your Higher Self. Through rest &

relaxation, you can find a renewal of your mind, body & spirit. When the moon is in your 12th house, don't repress your feelings or internal struggles. Allow yourself to process whatever is coming up for you. Listen to what your subconscious is trying to tell you – listen to your dreams, pay attention to what comes to the surface while meditating.

When the moon is in your 12th house, ask yourself:
- What is the deeper purpose to your life? What feels unaligned with this purpose?
- How can you relax & recharge at this time?
- What is coming to an ending in your life?

Tracking which house the moon is in for you each day can help you understand what area of your life you'll naturally be focusing on. This is most important for the new moons & full moons, although it is extremely helpful as a daily ritual.

As an example, let's say the new moon this month is in your 1st house of identity & self-awareness. Set your intentions this new moon to do with your appearance and your identity. The seeds you sow on the new moon will usually come full circle by the full moon in 6 months time, when the full moon falls in your 1st house – so by this time, whatever intentions you set for your appearance & identity should theoretically manifest into your reality.

For me, I've noticed that by focusing on the house each new & full moon falls in, it gives me greater clarity on what I should be focusing on manifesting – as it tells me what I'm naturally focused on anyway. We know that the moon in Gemini is a good time for being social & connecting with others, however Gemini falls in my 8th house of business, finances & shadow work. So when there's a new moon in Gemini, it would make sense for me to set intentions to connect with like-minded business owners, or write a book on making money. Do you see how I'm blending that sociable & communicative energy of Gemini with the energy of the 8th house?

So by using the house system, we can discover when the best times of the year are for working on certain projects. We can discover when it will be easier to manifest certain things, because that's what will be flowing for us naturally. Want to manifest a new home? Set your intentions for this new home when the new moon is in your 4th house. Want to manifest a soulmate?

Look out for the new moon in your 7th house. Manifesting new friends to hang out with? Too easy – work with the 11th house energy.

CHAPTER 10

Moon Manifesting Success Stories

So now that you've read all about HOW to manifest with the moon, I want to inspire you with real-life success stories from my community of moon manifesters!

"For a few years I had been looking at starting an Aromatherapy course. I had spent time researching the best colleges but couldn't seem to take that next step into signing up. Money was a bit tight, the timing didn't feel right, etc. Then this year in January on the day of the New Moon, I knew it was time to take the leap and I wrote down the intention to finally start the course. Surrounded by candles and crystals for manifesting, I visualised this dream coming true and then sent my wish out into the Universe for her to do her 'thing'. In the following few weeks, I received an email from the college I had been looking into. They were selling their courses at a huge discounted price! I immediately signed up, so thankful to the Universe for this new journey."

- *Belinda Moore from Perth, Western Australia*

"My husband and I were in need of some quick cash. We patiently waited for the full moon that week to appear, and when it did, we got right down to business - working on our manifesting moon magic! We set a $20 bill on a window seal in our house & set a rose quartz & selenite crystals on top of the $20 bill. Our goal was to bring love & clarity into our space to attract a divine cash flow into our bank accounts. We lit a candle & said a prayer to the universe to manifest our deepest wishes. The next morning we woke up to a call from my husband's parents. They explained how they saw us struggling a bit & wanted to gift us $5,000. My husband & I were brought to tears. Thank you, Universe!"

- *J from Redwood City, California*

"After months and months of troubles, with no money and no work, something started to shift as I made some practical decisions. On the 26th of May, with that powerful Full Moon + Eclipse combo, I went in the woods, I just sat on the bare ground, and stare at the moon in silence. I asked her to open a portal for me, and to radically change my life, instantly. I wanted to wake up the next day with a big shift. And I had it. The day after this manifestation, a very big fashion brand, for which I had interviewed, hired me, and the next day again I had a call for another job in the herbal medicine field. So in two days I filled a void that was getting bigger and bigger with two of the things I love the most, fashion and naturopathy. And this happened because I never ceased to manifest, I never ceased to trust in myself and the world, I never ceased to see and feel the magic in everything, and I always looked up at the moon as she was the Door to everything I wanted."

-    *Alice from San Marino*

"For 5 years I was working at a toxic work environment. I spent all my spare time desperately applying for a new job - I couldn't simply quit without another job to go to. I had always had a strong belief in tarot cards, so I turned my attention to the full moon to help manifest my dream of a new job. Over 2021 every full moon I'd make Moon Water with my Clear Quartz stones. One Full Moon after I finally had a job interview, I wrote on a sheet of paper "I work at the library and I am very happy". The glass was sat over with water and crystals inside. The day before I was due to get the call I drank the water to absorb the manifestation. I now work full time in a very happy new job."

-    *Alice Swain from Capel*

CHAPTER 11

Manifesting Tips For ANY Moon Phase

"Anyone can be a millionaire, but to become a billionaire you need an astrologer."
– J. P. Morgan

      I've been fascinated with the concept of manifesting since my early 20s. For me, manifesting represents a more feminine & intuitive method of creating wealth & abundance, as compared to the masculine model of structured income & rigid work hours. Manifesting opens a door that many of us never knew existed. There is MORE to life – and we are allowed to dream of creating a life of more abundance.

      I always kept myself small. Money was often tight when I was growing up, so from a young age I learnt how to be frugal & thrifty. During my early years of adulthood, I was always focused on saving money, always on the lookout for cheaper ways of living. I had a vision of growing all my own food so I'd never have to pay for ANYTHING ever again (I may have been forgetting about life's other expenses, but I had a dream!).

I manifested a lot of stuff. Free household appliances. Free food. Free furniture. The Universe kept providing for us – whatever we needed would just show up at the right timing!

But manifesting isn't all about free stuff showing up magically on your doorstep. Manifesting can help you set goals, and find the motivation to achieve them. Manifesting allows you to dream of bigger goals so you can keep aiming higher & live to your highest potential.

Sometimes manifesting means that you'll just bite the bullet and make that big purchase – like upgrading your computer or car, or booking that vacation. Setting your new moon intentions & goals is like making a promise to yourself. You'll fulfil that promise – but it would be nice if the Universe could help along the way! The point is, be prepared to do whatever it takes to achieve your new moon intentions. You can't just set your intentions and wait for them to manifest on their own.

I feel like I was asleep my whole life until I discovered moon manifesting. There is so much more purpose to my life now! I'm not just a whirlwind of chaos, without reason or a plan. I have goals – short-term & long-term. I've found balance in my life, by using the wheel of astrology as my guide.

I've found my own potential for showing up in the world, in ways that I never even DARED to dream of.

So, over my years of learning from different manifesting gurus & coaches, and experimenting with different manifesting practices, I've definitely found that some things work – and some things just haven't worked yet. I hope these tips help you understand more about manifesting – regardless of the moon phase.

Find Clarity

First up it's SO important to be really clear on what you want to manifest. Go deep into the specifics of your goal. If it's something tangible – get clear on what colour, shape, model, specifications or whatever other details are essential to you. When you are clear, specific and detailed about what you are asking for, then the Universe knows EXACTLY what to send you.

Sometimes when you set your intentions on the new moon, you might only have a small inkling of what you want to manifest. And that's okay! Keep building on your vision as you discover more about what you want to manifest.

Visualization is so helpful for getting into the finer details of what you want to manifest. Try a guided meditation to visualize your goals, or allow yourself to daydream for a while. You can also research – do an online search, or go window shopping. Try out products, get a closer look & feel. You'll soon have a clear vision of what you DO want – and you'll also be able to rule out what you DON'T want!

Take Aligned Action

I can't emphasize enough the importance of taking aligned action! I often see others who are trying to manifest their amazing dreams, but they get stuck when it comes to actually taking action towards achieving these goals.

I saw this A LOT when I was seeing clients as a herbalist, and I'm sure other health practitioners can agree. Often there are people who want to make big changes in their health, but they don't want to do the work. They don't want to change their eating habits, or exercise more, or stop smoking, or take prescribed herbal medicines or other supplements. People want a magic pill to solve their problems.

But there is no magic pill. The magic is within YOU. And you unlock this magic when you take aligned action.

Whether you're working on your health goals, financial goals, relationship goals, or manifesting something else into your life, you need to take action towards your goals. You can't send out your wishes and expect them to manifest miraculously.

Commit to your goals and continue to take action towards them EVERY DAY. Create a strategy to help you succeed – then follow that strategy. This is the NUMBER ONE method that I use to manifest my goals. A goal without a plan is just a dream. If you really do want to turn your dreams into reality, you need to roll up your sleeves and do the work to make it happen.

Just keep taking small steps towards your goals. Keep showing up every day, connecting with your goals and what you need to do to make it happen.

Declutter

Have you ever felt stuck? Perhaps abundance stopped flowing to you, or you couldn't seem to manifest your goals. You might have felt like you were attracting bad luck. Instead of manifesting money, you were manifesting bills. Instead of manifesting peace and love, you were manifesting arguments and chaos.

This can be a sign that decluttering is needed. Decluttering is one of the BEST ways to shift your energy. Physical clutter in your life can stagnate your energy. It's fascinating how clutter in our homes has an effect on other areas of our lives. I'm a huge believer in feng shui – you can explore more about this topic to discover how different areas of your home affect specific areas of your life, such as your relationships or wealth.

However, you don't need an understanding of feng shui to know that ANY clutter can affect your energy. Decluttering shifts your energy to allow MORE in your life. If you're holding onto stuff from your past, it can be really difficult to move forward a new path of abundance & prosperity. Letting go frees up space & energy for what you really want in your life.

Take a look at what you're holding onto. Are you keeping clothes that are a few sizes too small, waiting for the day that you'll be thin enough to wear them again? Are you keeping unwanted stuff that was given to you? Do you still have baby clothes in your cupboard – even though your youngest is now school-aged, and you're not planning to have another baby? Are you holding onto items from failed business ventures? Really LOOK at the clutter that's filling up your home – even if it's neatly tucked away in storage. Consider how the energy of this physical clutter is affected your own energy.

I used to hoard so much stuff (as I mentioned, I used to be quite frugal and thrifty, so I'd find ways to recycle all sorts of things!). I had boxes full of fabric scraps, art supplies, cardboard boxes and tubes, even old clothes that I planned to repurpose. I couldn't bear throwing stuff away – I saw the potential in almost everything!

But once I started getting serious about decluttering, I freed up so much energy. It was LIBERATING. And I rarely miss any of the stuff I decluttered.

The thing that really shifted in me was that I KNEW I could manifest this stuff back into my life whenever I needed it. If I needed more fabric or boxes or clothes, I could just manifest it!

As I became more confident in my ability to manifest, I also became more confident about decluttering. My standards became higher and I decluttered stuff that was broken, ugly, or just unaligned with my dream life. As I gained more clarity about the life I wanted to manifest, I gained more courage to declutter anything that didn't belong in this dream vision.

It's amazing how much we just "make do" with things that are broken, when we can easily and inexpensively replace them. Imagine how much your energy will shift when you're not feeling frustrated by chipped kitchenware, broken clothing or uncomfortable furniture! Sometimes it's the little things that keep our energy stuck. Upgrading these little things – like chipped mugs and broken bras – will help you FEEL more abundant. And that's what it's all about – shifting how you feel will help you manifest more easily.

Stay Positive

Negativity is one of the biggest factors that can hold you back from manifesting your desires. If you don't think you can achieve it, or you don't think you are worthy of receiving your desires, then you'll hold yourself back – consciously OR subconsciously.

Staying positive is the KEY to manifesting!

Expect positive outcomes. Always expect good things to happen! Your thoughts manifest into reality, so be mindful of what you're thinking. Catch yourself when you begin thinking negatively and reframe those thoughts into something more positive.

When we think negatively or expect negative outcomes, we manifest that into our lives. How many times have you thought something negative would happen – and it did? Worries and fears can creep into our minds and make us expect terrible things to happen. We MANIFEST those fears into our reality.

So what if you chose to manifest your dreams instead? What if you stopped thinking about the worst case scenario, and filled your mind with positive thoughts instead?

Positive affirmations are a wonderful tool for retraining your thoughts. You can create your own or find endless inspiration for affirmations on social media or the internet.

Some of my personal favourite affirmations are:

- I am a money magnet.

- I completely love and accept myself.
- I manifest good luck with ease.
- I attract positive opportunities.
- I have power to create change in my life.

A fun practice is to repeat an affirmation every morning. You can repeat the same affirmation every day, or pick a new one every day. At times I'll use oracle cards to inspire my morning affirmations, or I'll charge a crystal with my daily affirmation and carry that crystal with me for the day. When you remember throughout the day, repeat your affirmation. Soon it becomes second-nature to you, and you'll easily raise your vibes through the power of positive thoughts.

Detachment & Acceptance

Although we have big dreams & goals that we want to manifest, it's important to understand that the Universe works in mysterious ways, and sometimes we don't get what we want. Sometimes the Universe has something better for you, or sometimes we need to go through challenges & hardships FIRST so we can manifest our dreams later. Everything happens for a reason, so trust that things will work out – eventually.

Accept whatever happens. Be detached to the outcome. There's no point getting upset, frustrated or angry about the stuff you can't control. Practicing acceptance & detachment helps you to stay high vibe – even when times are tough.

So if you're trying to manifesting something and it doesn't happen, just accept that it didn't work out and try again. Don't feel disappointed – your disappointment will just bring your vibe down. Accept it, and move on.

It's helpful to view your goals as a curious experiment. Don't get emotionally attached to the outcome. Your happiness or self-worth doesn't depend on the success of your goals. You're just experimenting, and if it doesn't work the first time you can make adjustments and try again.

Try to be an "observer". Be objective about your goals and outcomes. Simply observe, as though you are a non-attached outsider. You could ask yourself some questions like: what were your goals? What actions did you take towards these goals? What happened? What could be improved for next time?

You can see much more clearly when you distance yourself a bit. Sometimes we get so caught up in our goals and trying to control the outcome that we lose sight of the bigger picture. Zoom out – you might pick up on insights that you missed during the manifesting process.

Gratitude

One of the strongest manifesting tools is gratitude. An open heart helps you receive more abundance into your life. Practice gratitude daily. Think about or write out a few things that you are grateful for EVERY day. Be specific too!

There's already a whole section about gratitude in the full moon chapter of this book, but it's so important to the manifesting process.

When we show gratitude, the Universe knows to send us MORE. What do you want more of? Show gratitude for every little thing that you want more of.

If there's something that you want to manifest, consider where it already is present in your life. Show gratitude for what's already present in your life, and watch it grow!

I feel that gratitude and staying positive go hand-in-hand, because showing gratitude helps you focus on the positive things in your life. Even if you feel like you always manifest bad luck, or that you're poor, or unhealthy, or unloved...gratitude will help you focus on where these self-beliefs are untrue. Gratitude will help you shift the perception that you have no money (because you're grateful for the coin you found on the ground) or that no one loves you (because you're grateful for the kindness that someone showed you today).

Keep your vibrations high through a daily dose of gratitude so you can easily manifest your desires into your life. Continually find things to be grateful for. Once you start listing out things to be grateful for, you'll find it hard to stop! There truly is so much to be grateful for in life.

About The Author

Kyra Howearth, founder of Herbal Moon Goddess, is an intuition & spirituality teacher based in New South Wales, Australia. Through her work, she aims to empower others through self-discovery & intuitive awareness. She teaches you how to discover your intuition & manifest your dreams with a blend of astrology, tarot, plant medicine & yoga.

When Kyra's not creating courses for the Herbal Moon Goddess Academy or meditating with her followers on Insight Timer, she's homeschooling her 4 children, spending time in her garden, or cooking delicious vegan food.

Join other moon manifesting lovers at the Herbal Moon Goddess Academy:
https://www.herbalmoongoddessacademy.com/

Website: https://herbalmoongoddess.com
Instagram: @herbal.moon.goddess
Facebook: Herbal Moon Goddess

Bonuses

Looking for more moon manifesting?

Don't forget to register for your book bonuses at *HerbalMoonGoddess.com/MoonManifestingBonus* so you can receive access to my New Moon Guided Meditation plus printable worksheets to help you use the wisdom from this book in a practical way.

You'll then receive regular updates from me so you can keep in touch with the current lunar energy and receive inspiration for how to harness the magick of the moon.